SWAHILI CHIC

SWAHILI CHIC
The Feng Shui of Africa

TEXT AND PHOTOGRAPHY BY
BIBI JORDAN

FOREWORD BY RICHARD LEAKEY

INSIGHT EDITIONS

IN ASSOCIATION WITH
EX MUNDO PRESS

TO NANCY GALLOWAY

safari guide extraordinaire

who shared with me the world of the Swahili

and

TO MY FRIENDS ON THE SWEET SWAHILI SHORES

Nawashukuru ghaya kwa msaada wenu. Mungu awabariki.

I ponder, if ever I would meet the traveler
Who has picked up the key
On some unknown seashore...
And she would open the door
which nobody could discover.

— Rabindranath Tagore, Bengali poet

Swahili Chic

Ex Mundo Press:
Designer: Linda Prescott
Editor: TrudiHope Schlomowitz
Digital Scans: BowHaus Digital Imaging

Insight Editions:
Publisher & Creative Director: Raoul Goff
Executive Directors: Michael Madden, Peter Beren
Art Director: Iain Morris
Executive Editor: Mariah Bear
Studio Production: Noah Potkin

INSIGHT EDITIONS

17 Paul Drive
San Rafael, Ca 94903
www.insighteditions.com
800.688.2218

Library of Congress Cataloging-in-Publication Data available.

ISBN 1-933784-16-4

Palace Press International, in association with Global ReLeaf,
will plant two trees for each tree used in the manufacturing
of this book. Global ReLeaf is an international campaign by
American Forests, the nation's oldest nonprofit conservation
organization and a world leader in planting trees for environmental restoration.

Insight Editions would like to thank Nam Nguyen, Marc Moore,
Barbara Genetin & Carina Cha.

Printed in China by Palace Press International
www.palacepress.com

10 9 8 7 6 5 4 3 2 1

SWAHILI CHIC
The Feng Shui of Africa

TEXT AND PHOTOGRAPHY BY
BIBI JORDAN

Foreword

The beautiful photographs in this book are a wonderful testimony to the skill and sensitivity of the author who has produced something that is quite different from the run of the mill publications on the Swahili culture in East Africa. It focuses on a subject little known in the West beyond academic spheres: the architecture of the Swahili stone towns. These stone towns extend along the entire length of the East African coastline from southern Tanzania northwards to Kenya, and beyond into Somalia.

The Swahili have been strongly influenced by Islam, introduced to the area in the late 9th century. But this is only one of many diverse elements that combined to create a unique Swahili style. Over the past thousand years, the Swahili have had contacts with many different people, Chinese, Indians, and Europeans, and Arabs interacted with Africans, producing a rich cultural tradition. The architecture in the stone town reflects this fascinating history.

Lamu, Mombasa, and Zanzibar are all towns that offer examples of Swahili design for stone buildings. Lamu may be the best example and this is well illustrated in the pages that follow. The feature of this work that I find of particular interest is the use of contemporary examples—residences that have been built afresh or old structures refurbished to provide modern living convenience. Some of these

examples are very beautiful, and having personally visited some, I can confirm that they are truly as comfortable and special as has been so eloquently described by the author.

It is strange and lamentable that so few contemporary architects in East Africa make use of historical design traditions. In the coastal towns of East Africa it is all too common today to see structures that are totally unsuitable for the local conditions. Ugly boxes using too much glass do nothing for the comfort of the occupants nor for the grace of a town's street facades. I can only hope that books such as this one will promote a realization that the past can be relevant, and the use of the ancient ideas in new contexts can be both pleasing and comfortable.

In historical times, there was no power for fans and electricity and the designers made every effort to maximise natural ventilation and cool rooms. With the energy crisis of the 21st Century and the exorbitant price of power, we should adapt to well-tested and proven concepts.

Another positive contribution that this book makes is to put forward a very positive aspect of Islam. In these days of terrorism and conflict, many westerners have unwittingly associated Islam with all things bad. This is both wrong and unfortunate. The

Swahili architecture now featured in new buildings and designs has been heavily influenced by Islam in ways that offer a sense of inner peace and beauty to which we can all relate. The modern homes illustrated and described so brilliantly in this book will underscore this point very effectively.

I hope that this volume will be studied by town planners and architects who will work on future projects along the coast of East Africa. A case in point that is indeed relevant relates to plans to build a new port and city infrastructure in Manda Bay to the north of Lamu. This essential undertaking could be all the more valuable if the planning authority insisted on an architectural design theme that reflected Swahili culture where ever practical. Residential housing, street facades in the business areas, and community facilities such as schools and hospitals could all be designed to give a very special identity to this city in the making. That would indeed be something to celebrate!

Richard Leakey

This is my purpose, this is my heart's design
To string pearls in a necklace, verse on verse
The great, pure pearls of Wisdom in the midst,
Small pearls of Thought a pendant down behind.
The Clasp I'll make by polishing my words
Arrange each gem in order where it fits...
[so that] the dark clouds of Ignorance dissolve
And, Wisdom's light and radiance blaze forth...

— *Sayyid Abdalla bin Ali bin Nasir, Swahili Poet
al-Inkishafi (Catechism of a Soul)*

ACKNOWLEDGMENTS

The awareness that human beings have an intellectual duty to explore other civilizations is a sentiment worthy of consideration today by all who wish to build a culture of respect for the global tribe into which we are evolving. In my travels, I seek to understand the soul of the culture and to uncover universal values. I follow the sensibility of the French artist Henri Matisse who said, "What I dream of is an art of balance, of purity and of serenity, devoid of troubling or depressing subject matter." Rather than being an objective account, *Swahili Chic* is a personal interpretation of voyages of wonder and magic along the Swahili coast. Far from being a comprehensive study, it is a teaser for a subject brimming with intrigue and controversy bound to engage the inquisitive reader but far beyond the scope of a coffee table book. *Swahili Chic* also presents only a few wonderful Swahili homes. Many were excluded to protect owners' privacy and others have recently been completed. CDs and DVDs offered on *www.bibijordan.com* include these latest additions.

I am indebted to Linda Prescott, an outstanding designer whose taste and expertise are also reflected in my website *www.bibijordan.com*. Linda and David Prescott were instrumental, too, in supplying additional photographs needed to complete the book. My deepest gratitude goes to BowHaus Digital Imaging in Los Angeles for superb digital scans, color corrections and client service with special mention to Kelly Coleman, Richard Eby and Nikki Kurtz. Sincere thanks go to Joe Berndt, who produced superb archival prints for the photo exhibit that complements this book and was launched by Joyce Maddox, curator with the Los Angeles City Cultural Center. Kenyan poet and Professor of Swahili Studies, Kineene wa Mutiso provided invaluable insights and constant encouragement as did Diana Smullens, Gesine Thomson, Michele Haney, Barbara DeWitt, and Jackie Karuleta. I have also been extremely fortunate to work with Palace Press, especially with my publisher Michael Maddon and his colleagues Iain Morris, Noah Potkin, and Mariah Bear. In East Africa special thanks go to Nancy Galloway, Naomi Cidi, Vintage Safaris, and Air Kenya.

Finally, I can never thank enough my wonderful parents and sisters for all they do for me. My children are the best of companions on my adventures abroad and through my life. And, last but not least, there is my own true love whose passion, humor and savoir faire makes all good things in life possible.

Bibi Jordan

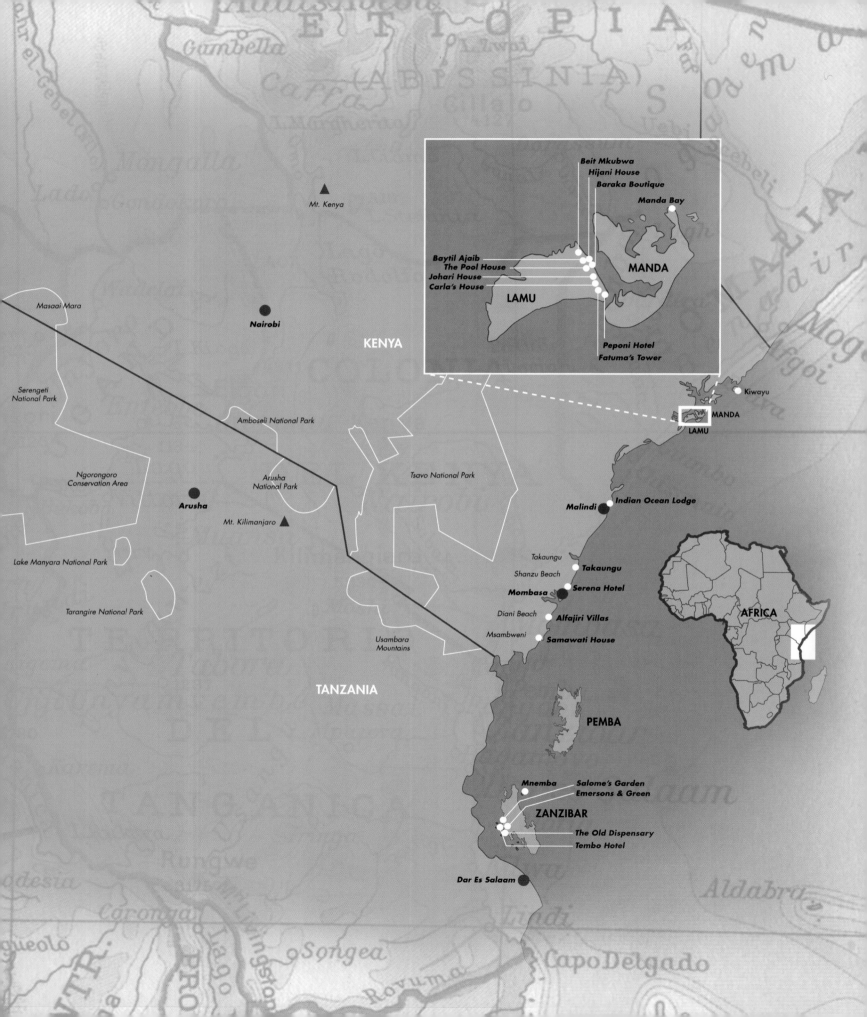

ET I OPIA

(ABISSINIA)

Gambella

Mt. Kenya

Masaai Mara

Serengeti
National Park

Nairobi

KENYA

Amboseli National Park

Ngorongoro
Conservation Area

Arusha
National Park

Tsavo National Park

Arusha

Mt. Kilimanjaro

Lake Manyara National Park

Tarangire National Park

Usambara
Mountains

TANZANIA

PEMBA

Mnemba

Salome's Garden
Emersons & Green

ZANZIBAR

The Old Dispensary

Tembo Hotel

Dar Es Salaam

Beit Mkubwa
Hijani House
Baraka Boutique

Manda Bay

Baytil Ajaib
The Pool House
Johari House
Carla's House

MANDA

LAMU

Peponi Hotel

Fatuma's Tower

Kiwayu

MANDA

LAMU

Malindi   Indian Ocean Lodge

Takaungu
Shanzu Beach   Takaungu

Mombasa   Serena Hotel

Diani Beach   Alfajiri Villas

Msambweni   Samawati House

AFRICA

CONTENTS

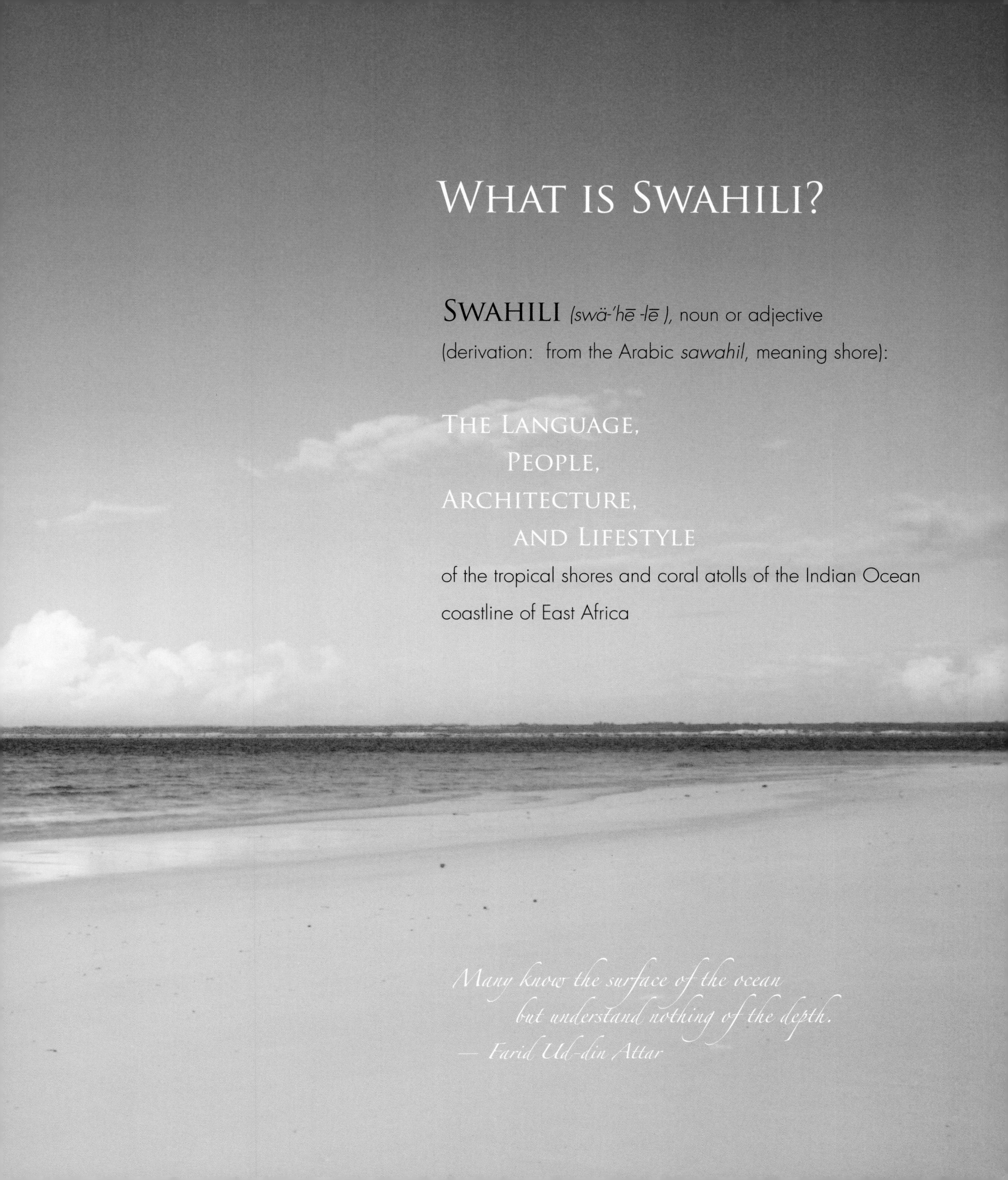

What is Swahili?

SWAHILI (*swä-'hē -lē*), noun or adjective

(derivation: from the Arabic *sawahil*, meaning shore):

THE LANGUAGE,
PEOPLE,
ARCHITECTURE,
AND LIFESTYLE

of the tropical shores and coral atolls of the Indian Ocean

coastline of East Africa

Many know the surface of the ocean
but understand nothing of the depth.
— Farid Ud-din Attar

SWAHILI *is...*

A LINGUA FRANCA

a trader's language combining

words from Africa, Arabia, Asia, and Europe

SWAHILI *is...*

A CULTURA FRANCA

a fusion culture melding

ideas from Africa, Arabia, Asia, and Europe

SWAHILI *is...*
AN URBANE TOWNSCAPE

Stone towns founded by traders and navigators
shaped by Islamic customs

SWAHILI *is...*
A RUSTIC SEASCAPE

Garden villages fashioned by farmers and fishermen
that shelter African traditions

SWAHILI *is...*
AN URBAN ARCHITECTURE
Townhouses built from blocks of coral

and framed with mangrove poles

SWAHILI *is...*
A RURAL ARCHITECTURE
Country cottages woven from leaves of palms

and cut from coconut trunks

SWAHILI *is...*

A SCHOOL OF THOUGHT

that transforms a city-state into a center of
cosmopolitanism, world learning, and integrity

SWAHILI *is...*

A SCHOOL OF DESIGN

that transforms a space into a sanctuary of
serenity, sensuality, and spirituality

You can't change the wind
But you can change the course.
— Swahili proverb

SWAHILI SHULE

Swahili. Derived from the Arabic *sawahil*, it literally means "of the shore." Many know it as the *lingua franca* of East Africa, a trading language that blends African, Arab, Asian, and European words. But Swahili is more than a language. It is also the *cultura franca* of Africa's Indian Ocean coastline, a traders' culture that combines elements of Africa and Arabia with East and West to produce a true cultural fusion.

The Swahili homelands are the tropical islands of Lamu, Mombasa, Malindi, and Zanzibar and the pristine coast of East Africa from Mogadishu in Somalia to Dar es Salaam in Tanzania. It is an Indian Ocean paradise: 300 miles of white beaches warmed to a constant 85 degrees by 10 hours of sunshine a day, tempered by the cooling Trade Winds.

I stumbled on this wonderful civilization years ago as a young backpacker. The memory of its charm beckoned me back as a photographer to document East Africa's wildlife and wild life. In my first book, *Safari Chic*, I focused on the savannah and the safari lifestyle of the interior. The East African coast and coral atolls are so unique, I realized they merited a book of their own.

Karibu (welcome) to *Swahili Chic*, my pilgrimage in search of Swahili style. Along the way I realized that this style, like the Chinese feng shui, is not limited to a school of design or a school of architecture: it also is a school of thought. To acknowledge this synergy, I refer to the Swahili aesthetic as Swahili shule—the Swahili school.

Swahili shule is expressed in a décor that harmonizes a home, creating a sanctuary of simplicity, spirituality, and sensuality. It is founded on a worldview that transformed ocean outposts into city-states of cosmopolitanism, world learning, and integrity.

This is a story little known in the West, but its time has come. We seek styles that celebrate ethnic diversity while uniting our global society. We long to tie traditions of the past with promises of the future. Like the Swahili, we aspire to impart a sense of dignity and balance to times of turmoil and trouble. This 2,000-year-old civilization may well offer helpful insights to a world moving uneasily into a new millennium.

Join me on a voyage of discovery as I take you to the Swahili Stone Towns to explore this fascinating style and then bring it home to the West, illustrating how anyone—whether in Malindi, Malibu, or Monaco —can transform a house into a haven of tranquility and personal growth with Swahili shule.

Swahili Shores – East Africa
Tides of History

The Swahili story is a saga of African kings, Chinese emperors, Indonesian cannibals, Omani sultans, Persian navigators, French pirates, Portuguese explorers, Dutch merchants, English missionaries, and American whalers. For thousands of years, traders from Asia and Arabia, borne on the northeast monsoon wind, the *Kazkazi*, arrived on the coral reef islands and tropical shores of East Africa. These lush equatorial islands, with their perennial sweet water, abundant citrus trees, fragrant spices, and voluptuous women seemed like a paradise to travelers after months at sea. The new arrivals sent intermediaries to bring trading goods from the interior while they lingered in the languid ocean outposts. Romances blossomed as exuberantly as the tropical flowers, soon bearing the fruit of a rich Swahili culture. They sailed home on the southerly wind, the *Kusi*, leaving behind beloved concubines, multiracial children, and new words from their languages. Each left a legacy, shaping the language, culture, architecture, and décor that is Swahili.

A thousand years before Europeans came to East Africa, the Swahili were known to our cultural fore-fathers. In 600 BC the Egyptian pharaoh Necho II dispatched Phoenicians from what is now Libya to circumnavigate Africa. During the Roman Empire, Greek navigators conducted a flourishing trade with Indian Ocean suppliers of spices, jewels, and ivory. By the first century there existed a guidebook to the East African coast called *The Periplus of the Erythraean Sea*. With the collapse of classical civilization in Europe, contact with the Swahili was lost to the Western world.

Rome fell, but the Swahili city-states prospered, becoming as powerful a mercantile bloc as the Mediterranean became in the Renaissance. Like a string of pearls that adorn a graceful neck, a line of Swahili principalities created by consecutive waves of settlers dotted the East African coastline from Mogadishu to Madagascar. Bantu people migrating from Central Africa encountered Indonesians arriving in outrigger canoes. Persian royalty trailblazed new coastal settlements in the wake of Arab traders in seaworthy *dhows* and Chinese explorers in fleets of enormous junks called Star Rafts.

While Europe sank into the Dark Ages, plundered by Huns, Franks, Vandals, Turks, Goths, and Saxons, the Swahili soared into a peaceful Golden Age. Unlike Europeans, many of whom subsisted in dank hovels

without sanitation, the Swahili patricians flourished in an affluent, literate, and cosmopolitan environment. Tenth-century Arab traveler Abu Hasan Ali al-Mas'udi observed how wealthy Swahili lived in flat-roofed three-story Stone Houses featuring bathrooms with plumbing, balconies with glazed windows, and interiors with plastered walls. Brass-studded front doors opened onto chambers covered with Persian rugs and wall niches filled with Chinese porcelain and Venetian glass.

Marco Polo's contemporary, Ibn Battuta, reported that the Swahili city of Kilwa was "amongst the most beautiful and elegantly built" of the cities he had seen in Europe, Asia, and Africa. He was dazzled by the ruler's huge estate, which boasted a horizon swimming pool and such a profusion of fine china dishes that they were wantonly plastered into the external walls.

The Swahili ingeniously harnessed the natural resources of the coastal ecosystem to establish the communities that endure today. With blocks carved from terrestrial coral and poles cut from the littoral mangroves, they erected tiered towns on hilly promontories. These Stone Towns (a misnomer, as they were built of coral) were labyrinths of narrow corridors formed by the adjoining whitewashed walls of majestic townhouses that harbored stately patricians and their harems.

These early Swahili patricians were ambitious developers who sought to profit through the steady expansion of their mercantile network. In the process, they spread and adapted the *utamaduni* (cosmopolitanism) and *ustaarabu* (world learning) of their Islamic culture in Arabia and Persia. Their solid homes with thick walls and slit windows were designed as bastions of privacy, shielding their families from the stress and stares of commercial life. Considered by historians as the most important legacy of the Swahili, the Stone Houses nurtured fundamental Swahili values of *ushwari* (calm), *usafi* (purity), and *uzuri* (sensuality).

But as a Swahili proverb advises, "If the farmer grew no crops, the scholar could not study." The Swahili Stone Town culture would never have blossomed had it not been supported by the *shamba* (garden) villages of the outlying island towns. These rural communities provided the fresh fruit, agricultural produce, and abundant seafood that nourished the Stone Towns. Using thatch woven from palm fronds and trunks felled from coconut trees, the villagers built rustic homesteads flanked with generous garden plots and encircled with well-irrigated fields.

Just as the Stone Houses preserved the community's Islamic heritage, the Shamba Homes sheltered indigenous Bantu traditions known as *mila*. These traditions are the source of a key value incorporated into the Swahili persona: *ungwana*, or integrity, that requires adherence to a noble code of ethics incorporating honor, hospitality, and decorum. From *mila* also come *uganga* (shamanism), *mizimu* (ancestor spirits), and *dawa* (herbal medicine). These complemented the Islamic heritage of the Stone Towns with a rich African spiritual inheritance.

Whether living in the urban Stone Houses or the rural Shamba Homes, the Swahili were essentially middlemen. As the hub of the busy Indian Ocean Trade Winds network, the Swahili city-states were entrepôts for traders from Arabia, Persia, India, and China who sailed the seas to exchange their cargoes of silk, brocade, glass, spices, and china for ivory, skins, gold, and ambergris from Africa.

But the tides did not bring only peaceful traders. For over one thousand years, rich Swahili towns like Malindi and Mombasa were inundated by waves of foreign powers lusting for ports from which to control the lucrative spice trade. The Indonesians, Portuguese, Turks, Omanis, Germans, and British all made their play at the Swahili coast.

Inadvertently in the 18th and 19th centuries, the coast became the seat of a naval empire. Enchanted by Zanzibar, the Sultan of Oman relocated the seat

of the Omani sultanate from the barren shores of Muscat to the fertile island, establishing plantations of cloves, a spice that commanded a price equal to its weight in gold. These riches financed the urban development of Zanzibar by Indian artisans who crafted opulent palaces, lavish harems, and cosseted Persian baths.

Adept in their role as middlemen, the Swahili absorbed elements from each new culture while still retaining their own identity. Like the coral reefs rooted in the ocean floor that withstood the monsoon tides, the Swahili survived the sway of foreigners while remaining secure in their own traditions. Each wave, however, left an imprint, creating today's distinctive Swahili culture. Expressing a multiplicity of traditions and interactions, Swahili shule is relevant to today's task of building an enlightened global community through dialogue and discovery.

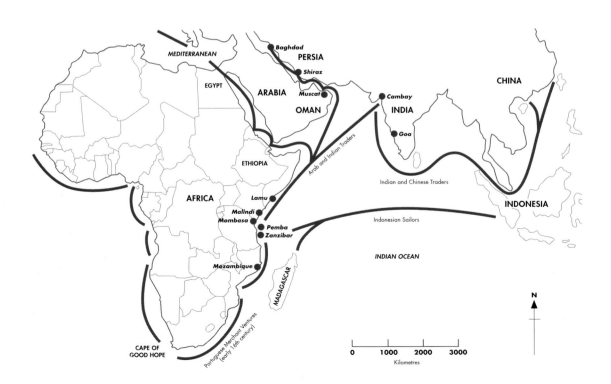

Stone Houses

CORAL TOWNHOUSES – MKOMANI STONE TOWN
STONE HOUSES

Swahili shule is to Africa as feng shui is to Asia. Both express a design philosophy that balances the exterior environment with the internal spirit. Like a zen style, it is a school of thought that can be applied to interior design by anyone who wants to inject a simple aesthetic and reserved elegance into daily living.

The distinctive Swahili style is nowhere better expressed than the Stone Town of Lamu, a small island city-state on the Indian Ocean coast of northern Kenya. Built by the wealthy patricians whose ancestors founded Lamu, Mkomani features hundreds of coral mansions, also called Stone Houses, hidden within a maze of indistinguishable passageways.

Until recently, conservation in Africa focused nearly entirely on wildlife. Except in Egypt, African architecture was not deemed worthy of preservation. That changed when the United Nations Educational, Scientific, and Cultural Organization (UNESCO) designated Mkomani a World Heritage Site in 2004. Savvy European and African designers descended on this cool, shady *mtaa* (quarter) to renovate its endangered coral architecture into historic homes and travelers' inns for a wealthy international clientele.

The Stone Houses of Mkomani are quite distinct from Egyptian temples, but there exist interesting parallels. Both are considered among the most important legacies of their respective cultures. Both are built according to a uniform layout. And both are the manifestation of a family's sense of permanence in terms of status, proprietorship, and ancestry.

In their layout and furnishings, the Stone Houses reflect Islamic values of seclusion and scholarship. They also evoke elements of Asian décor. Like Chinese feng shui or Indian vastu shastra, Swahili shule is based on an axial plan. The Swahili house, like the Swahili mosque, has a north-south orientation reflecting the importance of Mecca, which is situated due north. As Usam Ghaidan points out in his excellent reference book *Lamu: A Study of the Swahili Town*, this axis serves as an "intimacy gradient" so that rooms become darker, yet more intimate and more ornate, as the visitor ventures deeper into the dwelling.

Navigating a warren of alleyways just wide enough for a fully laden donkey to pass, the traveler is easily disoriented by the continuous corridors of unadorned plaster walls joining three-story townhouses. Every street and every house appears the same. This was precisely the aim of the Swahili patricians, who wished to instill a sense of conformity and equality within their community. The dignified, uniform exterior of the Stone House paralleled the dignified but unpretentious *kanzu* (long white robe) worn by the patricians themselves.

Both were expressions of *ungwana*, an ethic of noble conduct that required Swahili to comport themselves in a manner appropriate to their status. As the elite, the patricians were obliged to speak, dress, and dwell virtuously. Inherent in this concept was the understanding that social status should be based on sound character rather than on financial assets or family lineage. Fortune and heritage were *baraka*, blessings from God, not to be flaunted but to be guarded with respect and humility.

The intimacy gradient was another expression of *ungwana*. The Swahili differentiate between public areas, regarded as male, and private areas, regarded as female. The street is considered a male space where it is inappropriate for a woman to show her face. The Swahili woman's *buibui* (black cloak) provides the symbolic anonymity required to maintain not only personal *heshima* (honor) but also the honor of the family and the community. Originally introduced to differentiate upper-class women from slaves, the *buibui* was embraced following abolition, by freed slaves and the lower classes as an equal right.

The unadorned coral plaster walls of Lamu's tall dwellings shade narrow alleyways from the equatorial sun. Recessed porches are lined with baraza (stone benches) where casual acquaintances can be entertained. This is the most public area of the very private Swahili Stone House.

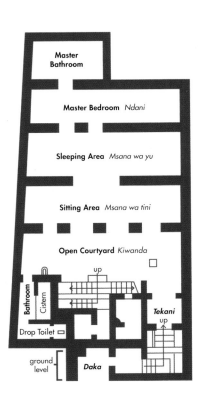

After the street, the next most public area is a recessed front porch of the Stone House called the *daka*. Located on the north side of the house, the *daka* is raised above the cobbled street and is a step up from the street on the intimacy gradient. The shaded interior and subdued colors provide a comfortable transition from the bustle of the open street to the seclusion of the home's interior. Flanked with a *baraza* (stone bench), the *daka* is a semi-public gathering space, like a New York City brownstone stoop, where acquaintances stop to chat, young men play checkers, and wizened elders gather to philosophize.

At the back of the *daka* is the door to the house. Ornately carved from valuable hardwood and studded with brass tacks, these impressive entrances are the only concession to ornamentation on the building's exterior. Contrasting with the unadorned exterior walls and the simple lines of the *daka*, these majestic doors boldly proclaim the homeowner's aspirations with designs that symbolize fortune, love, and health. As the explorer Richard Burton remarked in 1857, "the higher the tenement, the bigger the gateway, the heavier the padlock and the huger the iron studs that nail the door of heavy timber, the greater is the owner's dignity."

Few foreigners enter these doors, as the Stone Houses are fortresses of privacy and reserve. On the other hand, donkeys are seen nonchalantly stepping over the threshold into the ground floor. A dark cavern, this floor is for animals and servants. A steep staircase leads to the second and third stories, which are reserved for the family.

Inquisitive visitors used to be limited to stealing a glimpse through a door left ajar or an unshuttered window, but now exclusive guest houses provide access beyond the public *daka* into the private chambers of the coral villas. The Lamu Museum's renovated Stone House also provides insights into the lifestyle of the rich patricians of the Swahili Golden Age.

Climbing halfway up the staircase of a typical Stone House, the visitor arrives at the *sebule,* the guest room. The staircase continues up to a covered landing, the *tekani.* This reception area is as far as any male guest can penetrate because the remaining area is reserved for family members and women. A narrow window strategically placed above eye level fills the area with soft light while shielding the interior from the eyes of curious neighbors. High ceilings with dark rafters and whitewashed walls bordered by a frieze of carved plaster create a stately atmosphere in the small antechamber.

Beyond the *tekani* is an atrium courtyard called the *kiwanda.* It is a center of activity where children play and servants work. Open to the sky, the *kiwanda* provides ventilation and lighting that compensate for the lack of windows. A second staircase, too steep for small toddlers, leads to the third floor where the *kidara cha meko* (rooftop kitchen) is located. A penthouse veranda shaded by a palm-thatch roof provides a sitting area for women to enjoy the breeze while chatting across rooftops to friends. Facing the *kiwanda* are the three rectangular landings called *msana* (galleries) that constitute the main living space of the house.

Spanning the width of the house, each is approximately 10 feet deep. Stacked parallel, each slopes gently towards the courtyard and is a step higher than the next so that when the floors are washed, water cascades easily into the *kiwanda,* tumbling down to street gutters that cant to the sea.

Looking onto the courtyard is the first gallery, called the *msana wa tini.* A shallow sitting area, it provides shade without compromising the view of the sky. It is delineated by square columns called *zipiya* that are embellished with delicate carved lines that give grace to their substantial girth.

The second, more private gallery, *the msana wa yuu,* is divided into three sections. At both ends are identical sleeping alcoves, separated by a central sitting area. A modicum of privacy is provided by closing the bright curtains hung on intricately turned wooden poles *(miwandi).* In the past, these sleeping alcoves contained stacks of nested cots in various sizes made from simple wooden frames on which were lashed mats of plaited coconut coir. They were brought out to use as divans or beds as needed. Later, the more formal *pavilao* bed was introduced by Goan craftsmen accustomed to replicating Portuguese furniture for their colonial masters. This was a bed so high that a low bench *(ntaanyao)* was provided to allow access to family members, while barring unwelcome pests.

The central sitting area separating the two alcoves is traditionally furnished with two formal chairs built of dark mahogany and inlaid with mother-of-pearl. These "chairs of power" were reserved for the proprietor or were moved to the *tekani* for esteemed guests. Like the Stone House itself, the décor of the galleries is simple and symmetrical.

Stacked one behind the other, the narrow galleries have the potential to become increasingly gloomy, but the oppressiveness inherent in the layout is

The Lamu Museum's Stone House recreates the lifestyle of the rich Swahili patricians. Two galleries on the south, or private, side of the house provide sleeping areas. One of them contains two symmetrical alcoves. In the last gallery, the master bedroom is decorated with splendid zidaka (wall niches) that exude inner peace.

brilliantly counteracted by luminous white coral plaster carvings that become progressively grand. A final step up leads through a heavy door into the third and most private space. This is the parents' bedroom, or *ndani* (inner) room. It serves as a showcase of exquisite coral carvings and ornamental niches displaying china plates, glass vessels, and leather-bound books from faraway lands.

All this, however, is modest compared to the magnificent en suite bathroom decorated with elaborate plasterwork and niches. A trifoliate arch discretely separates a drop toilet from the bathing area, where a cistern of water reveals a china bowl placed in its depth to ensure that a well of water always remains for the tiny fish kept to eliminate mosquito larvae. As the Japanese do before soaking in a hot tub, the Swahili bathe by dousing their bodies with a small bucket; thus they avoid polluting the cistern. Splashes of wastewater drain down to street gutters through channels chiseled in the bathroom floor.

This simple layout characterizes the homes within the Stone Town of Lamu. The outer public face of the house is humble. Sheltered within strong walls is a private interior rich with family life, heirlooms, and libraries. The majestic elevation of the courtyard, the orderly symmetry of the galleries, and the luminescence of the inner sanctum provide a sense of purity and peace that define the ideal Swahili patrician and the quintessential Stone House.

*If the house is to be set in order, one cannot
begin with the present; he must begin with the past.*
— *John Hope Franklin*

QUINTESSENTIAL STONE HOUSE
BEIT MKUBWA

Beit Mkubwa, "The Big House" is a 19th-century Stone House restored to its original glory by Bo van der Assum. A corporate lawyer for the Dutch airline KLM, Bo was traveling to Madagascar when a cancelled connection in Nairobi resulted in an unplanned sojourn in Lamu. The detour changed his holiday and his life. He bought a dilapidated Stone House, which had been subdivided into apartments, from an absentee owner who preferred the luxury of a new home in a modern resort. Bo converted the old house back to the traditional Swahili layout, revitalizing ancient building and carving techniques on the verge of demise. Determined to furnish his two homes in true Swahili style, Bo launched a local workshop that exports Lamu tables and beds to his New York headquarters while his Swahili manager, Ali, oversees the exclusive Lamu guest house with his young nephew, Abdullah. A world traveler, Bo considers the island his favorite retreat. ***"No other place holds such power of fascination," he says. "Only Lamu."***

above top :: The simple *daka* (recessed porch) at the front of the house and the delicately carved entrance to the master bedroom at the back delineate the most public and most private areas of the house. **above bottom** :: Two alcoves offer sleeping areas on the roof and the main floor.

right :: Niches in the wall adjacent to the master bedroom were used by Swahili patricians to display treasures from overseas.

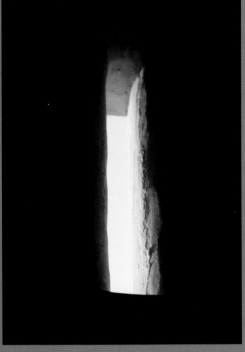

above :: A solid block of wood turned on a lathe produces a sturdy but stunning table leg from Lamu Industries' workshop.

left :: The rooftop landing looks down onto the central courtyard of the interior, which provides ventilation and illumination for the second floor. In the olden days, evaporation of water seeping through clay pots provided natural refrigeration.

above :: Typical Stone House windows are fortress-like slits that protect privacy and control interior temperature.

above :: Walls covered in coral plaster are chiseled into fine graceful geometric patterns that provide relief from the uniform dimensions of the interior galleries.

above :: Showcasing the fine woodwork of the Swahili is an elegant side table displaying an antique brass coffeepot and tea samovar. Three center posts from discarded doors are decorated with patterns that symbolize the homeowner's aspirations.

right :: Facing the central courtyard, the first gallery is used as a Western-style dining area. It features a Lamu table made of *mbambakofi*, a hardwood resembling mahogany. The two piers and background wall are covered with carved coral plaster, which introduces an airy element to the depths of the house.

He who hath drunk of Africa's fountains,
will drink again.
— Arab proverb

*The strength of a nation is derived
from the integrity of its homes.
— Confucius*

THE HOUSE OF WONDER
BAYTIL AJAIB

"Renovating a Swahili Stone House renewed my own soul," says Abdul Malik Bilal speaking of his palatial townhouse "House of Wonder." Born in Detroit as Paul Weaver, he was raised in Orlando with 9 siblings and then spent his adolescence in Paris with his Dominican grandparents. Retiring from a banking career in Germany, he and his business partner, Norbert Herget, joined the wave of visionaries who, in anticipation of Lamu's designation as a UNESCO World Heritage Site, swept down the Indian Ocean coastline. While others were satisfied with converting coral houses into seaside havens, Malik also converted himself into a Swahili patrician. He embraced Islam, the Swahili dress, and the Stone House lifestyle. All three are essential to achieve *usafi* (purity), a defining concept of the Swahili character. Adorning the body with a clean pressed white *kanzu* (long shirt) and an embroidered *kofia* (skull cap) and decking the home with carved white plaster and simple stately furnishings are acts of purification that mirror the adage; **"Cleanliness is next to godliness."**

above left :: Ceiling rafters are stained in the traditional colors of burgundy and black, using natural dyes made from pomegranate and ash. **lower left** :: A headboard of fine spindles demonstrates the workmanship of Indian carpenters hired by colonists to duplicate European styles. **right** :: Windows have been added to the sleeping alcove to provide additional lighting that filters through a romantic canopy of mosquito netting. High beds called *pavilao* are reached using stepping stools.

Ancestors, ancestors, guide me to whatever
I'm looking for, whatever it may be.
—Ethiopian proverb

above :: Situated on the left side (the side considered unclean), the toilet is accessed through a trifoliate arch, an arch form also characteristic of Swahili mosques. The cistern is filled from a rooftop reservoir through an elaborate system of internal aqueducts. Scented candles and incense dispel bad spirits called *habisi* that haunt latrines.

left :: The bathrooms of Swahili Stone Houses have not only had efficient plumbing for many centuries, they are also exquisitely decorated with delicate carved coral plaster that denotes moral purity. This creates an environment well suited to the ritual cleansing that Muslims must perform before each of the five daily prayers.

above and right : Toward the back of the house, the walls of the most intimate areas feature niches or *zidaka* surrounded by intricate carvings of coral plaster. These niches are used to display treasures, especially antiques and books from Persia, Arabia, India, and China. The Stone House becomes, in essence, a treasure house of cosmopolitanism *(utamaduni)* and world learning *(ustaarabu)*. Fine furniture, exquisite coral plaster, and objets d'art are the outward expression of a family's antiquity and provenance.

No one can see their reflection in running water;
It is only in still water we can see.
— The Wisdom of the Taoist

AN OASIS OF CALM
POOL HOUSE

An oasis of calm, the Pool House was created by Jann-Henrik van Leeuwen, an international consultant at the World Bank in Washington, DC. The name is derived from the swimming pool located in the area conventionally designated as the *kiwanda* (central courtyard). Soft light reflects from the pool into the wide doorways of the galleries, and air cooled by the water floats through the interior. Just as feng shui harmonizes home with environment, **Swahili style makes use of the natural resources of sun, wind, and water.** There is a serene calm *(ushwari),* spiritual purity *(usafi),* and sensual beauty *(uzuri).* These are qualities of East Africa's 2,000-year-old school *(shule)* of design and philosophy described as Swahili shule. Like Zen, the Swahili worldview is not a religion but a philosophy that can be applied to interior design to create equilibrium and tranquility. Yet it cannot be simply absorbed by the mind. As the Swahili mystics teach, understanding can be achieved only by taking the time **"to see with the eyes of the heart."**

above upper left :: A headboard provides an intriguing grill for an exterior window set in a wall of coral rag. **above lower left** :: Designs from Indonesia have been incorporated into the headboard of the master bedroom. **above right** :: Elaborate spindlework on the headboard reflects Indian influence in Lamu workshops.

far right :: The blue-and-white motif of the bed linen and china were inspired not by the owner's Dutch heritage but by the Swahili's affinity for the classical Chinese ceramics that arrived on trading junks in the 15th century.

above :: The recessed soap dish reflects the traditional turtle shape of the wall niche carved in coral plaster.

above :: The pit toilet has been upgraded to a flush toilet and is flanked by a chair dubbed the "throne of power."

above :: In a nearby alcove, a classic wall niche, or *zidaka*, is carved from coral plaster in the stylized shape of a sea turtle.

left :: The cistern has been replaced by a modern bathtub, shower, and sink. A marble bench inspired by the Swahili *baraza* is a contemporary adaptation of a traditional design.

upper left and lower right :: The selective use of fine furnishings and exotic accessories create an authentic Swahili look of mystery and charm.

lower left and upper right :: Lanterns designed by the homeowner and made in India cast intriguing patterns around the pool at night.

Their lighted mansions glowed with lamps of brass
and crystal till night seemed like very day.
— Sayyid Abdalla bin Ali bin Nasir, Swahili poet

SHOPFRONT HOMES - LAMU MARKET
TRADING PLACES

SHOPFRONT HOMES - LAMU MARKET
TRADING PLACES

Lamu is a town, an island, and an archipelago that gives the impression of stepping back in time. Visitors sail into town aboard a *jahazi*, the potbellied dhow that shuttles them from the sandy airfield of nearby Manda Island to the Lamu quay, where sloe-eyed donkeys wait to transport backpacks and dive bags. Dhows and donkeys remain the only transportation in Lamu town, island, and archipelago.

As the creaking boat plies across the channel, Lamu's skyline materializes. The bustling quay is lined with warehouses, cafés, and colonial-era residential buildings. Behind, stacked in tiers up the hill, are the stately Stone Homes of the Lamu patricians in the Mkomani Stone Town. The *makuti* (thatch) cottages of the working class nestle at either end of the waterfront. At the far end, just out of sight, is the village of Shela, another island haven of Swahili Stone Houses.

For thousands of years, Lamu has been a busy port with a constant influx of traders, sailors, and laborers. Even today the wharf, the sea promenade, and the marketplace teem with Bajuni fishermen, Yemeni traders, Goan tailors, Indian merchants, Ceylonese jewelers, Omani silversmiths, and European dilettantes. In contrast to the hushed, shaded Stone Town, this section is brash and blazing. The Stone Town may be the heart of Lamu, but the market streets are the capillaries through which circulate the life force of the community.

Like the Stone Houses, Swahili harbor towns are basically uniform in plan. The main street, the *ndia kuu*, dissects the town, much as the *decumannus* (central road) did in the Roman city-ports. While the Stone Town is exclusive and elusive, the main street is inclusive and effusive. The street is lined on both sides with deep, narrow shops where locksmiths and carpenters, grocers and herbalists, antique dealers and fabric importers, fishmongers and bakers beguile passerbys with a welcoming *"Karibuni."* Donkeys clatter down cobbled streets and hand-pulled wooden carts clack past pedestrians sampling the wares of sidewalk vendors. A medley of aromas waft from food stalls offering roasted corn on the cob, vegetarian samosas, fish kebabs, coconut donuts, and sticky halwa.

Patrician women, sequestered by day in the privacy of the Stone Houses, flock out at dusk into the market streets. Draped in the all-encompassing black *buibui* that can be swept across the face with a surprising air of flirtation, the women mass inside jewelry shops glittering with the latest temptations from India and Ceylon. Their men gather on the market's stone benches, elegantly dressed in *kanzu* robes scented with frankincense, and drink endless demitasses of thick spiced coffee while brokering business deals.

The Swahili patricians served as middlemen between traders from overseas and suppliers from the hinterland. They assiduously avoided banal work beneath their dignity. This left ample jobs for other settlers —an opportunity seized by various immigrant groups, each with its own specialization. Hadrami Muslims from the area that is now Yemen were employed as water carriers, porters, and seamen. Indian Muslims sold fabric from India and the American colonies. Bohra Muslims from Gujarat on the northwest coast of India were locksmiths and watchmakers who often opened hardware stores. They were also accomplished journeymen, renowned for their metal and wood work.

Indian Hindus were also prominent players. Unlike Islam, the Hindu faith allows profit-making on loans and precious metals, so the Hindus became Lamu's bankers and jewelers. Indian Christians from the Portuguese colony of Goa worked as tailors, bakers, and civil servants.

Visitors to Lamu are taxied to town aboard a dhow, giving them an excellent view of the town with its busy waterfront. The Stone Town houses are hidden behind narrow alleyways, while at the far end of the quay are simple dwellings of makuti *(palm thatch) and coral rag, home to common folk.*

Living harmoniously with the Lamu patricians but residing in the market area instead of the Stone Town, the Hindu shopkeepers and Gujarati artisans created a distinctive architecture that has more in common with a Bombay bazaar than an Arabian covered market. The Hindu religion does not dictate seclusion of women, so there was no compulsion to separate business and home. Houses did not need to be oriented toward Mecca, so they could have an east-west axis. As a result, the main street in the Lamu market area is conveniently located parallel to the waterfront and is lined with shopfront homes with residential quarters located above the stores.

The homes here have a style distinct from that of the Stone Houses. Instead of being a windowless three-story building, the typical market house is a two-story structure with shuttered windows. The shop entrance features a large wooden door flanked by two shop windows. The doors display an idiosyncratic Gujarati style with a carved center post. Lacking the ornamented lintel and frame of the Stone House door, they are decorated with squared stile and rail panels embellished with protruding brass bosses. The shop front is whitewashed, with a long *baraza* running the length of the facade.

The ground floor layout consists of three narrow rooms. The first room accommodates a small shop and the next two are large storerooms. Because of the monsoon, shipments tended to be infrequent, so ample space had to be reserved for storage.

A small plain door on the side provides the outside entrance to a narrow stairway that leads to the family quarters above. A small central interior courtyard, sometimes adorned with arched columns, provides light and ventilation for the home. At the front of the house directly above the shop is a reception room, with shuttered windows often set in recessed niches, overlooking the street. More lavish homes boast the addition of an elaborate wooden or wrought-iron balcony cantilevered from the first floor and projecting over the street to shade the *baraza* below where shoppers stop to rest.

An Indian influence is also seen on the veranda homes lining the seaside promenade. They were built as homes for wealthy merchant families hailing from Oman, India, and Zanzibar. Adjacent and parallel to the main street, they also have an east-west orientation and are characterized by an upper-story balcony extending the full length of the facade. Larger houses have six or seven bays supported by massive pillars, forming a classic stone arcade that provides a transition between the public quay and the private home. Smaller houses have three or four bays bolstered by wooden balustrades. Both have long shuttered windows that open to impressive views of the sea. Intricate latticework trellises screen the balcony from the bustle below while giving free access to the sea view and the breeze. With its outward orientation, lavish woodwork, and ornate crenellated rooftop, the veranda house has more in common with 19th-century buildings in seaports around the Indian Ocean than with the Stone Town.

The main street of Lamu's market area is a busy thoroughfare of commerce and conversation. Wazee (elders) gather on baraza to chat. No motorized vehicles are allowed on Lamu, so the only means of locomotion is by foot or by donkey. Transportation of heavy goods relies on large wooden carts pulled by hand.

Architecturally, the commercial districts of the market and the quay reflect Indian and Omani influences. Culturally, they are manifestations of two key qualities of the Swahili character: *utamaduni* (cosmopolitanism) and *ustaarabu* (world learning). *Utamaduni* is derived from the Arabic word *medina*, which means city. Arab cities like Medina, Jerusalem, Damascus, Baghdad, and Granada were urbane centers that, like the Swahili city-states, attracted traders and travelers around the world from Iberia to China. The Swahilis' success as middlemen was dependent on their ability to understand foreign cultures and to engage in intercultural dialogues—hence the emphasis on cosmopolitanism.

Ustaarabu, derived from the Arabic word for learning, refers to both academic and spiritual wisdom. Swahili society was as devoted to the belles lettres as the French and as open-minded toward religion as America has historically been. A Jewish traveler to the area noted that "there are many people of all religions in this city, and nobody is allowed to insult their religions." An early Chinese voyager in AD 762 reported that the Swahili towns included observers of three religions: Monophysite Christianity, Islam, and traditional African religion. Lamu, in particular, had a local Sufi brotherhood of Islamic mystics—free-thinkers who were not confined to dogma. To make religion accessible to the poor and illiterate, they introduced rituals with musical instruments such as tambourines and drums that accompanied rhythmic swaying and chanting. They taught that the world's religions could be compared to patterns cast by different screens in front of a single source of light. Observers could choose any pattern to contemplate but should discern that the source of illumination for all was the same.

The Indian influence is apparent in the balconies that characterize the storefront homes and the even more lavish balconies of the veranda houses on the seafront promenade. In a departure from characteristic simplicity and privacy of the Stone House, these balconies are lavishly decorated with fretwork, giving a whimsical touch of Hindu fantasy.

The value placed on cosmopolitanism and world learning in Swahili ethics acknowledges the immigrant communities who shared with East Africa their lifestyles and worldviews. This sensibility is reflected in the learned texts, art objects, and fine fabrics from around the world that are displayed in niches and draped over beds, divans, and rods in Swahili homes. Secure in their own beliefs, the Swahili invited a material and spoken exchange between nationalities, perceiving that knowledge of others could only add depth to their own society.

Fortune is not owned by right;
It is a gift that has been given.
— Swahili proverb

SHOPFRONT HOME OF FORTUNE
BARAKA BOUTIQUE

"Ever since I was a child, I always wanted to live in Africa and make an artistic contribution," says Kate Baumgarten. An Australian jewelry designer and art dealer, Kate came to Lamu in the 1960s to open a craft boutique. She invented a shop name, *Baraka*, which she subsequently learned was an authentic Swahili word. Meaning a blessing from God, it connotes fortune in both senses of the English word: luck and wealth. Now one of Lamu's leading environmental and cultural activists, Kate is fondly referred to as *Mama Baraka* in recognition of the opportunities she has created for the community. From her living quarters above the shop, she oversees a number of enterprises including a charming coffeeshop, a chic restaurant, and an artisan cooperative. Her home illustrates how Swahili shule can create a haven of *ushwari* (serenity), *usafi* (spirituality), and *uzuri* (sensuality) in the midst of the bustling market environment.

above :: A carved niche *(zidaka)* surrounded by exquisitely carved white coral plaster offers a spiritual focus for this secluded meditation corner.

right :: Draped canvas creates a tent-like ceiling enhanced by the dreamy diaphanous mosquito netting that encloses the Balinese bed.
On either side, low Indian chairs complete a distinctive Trade Winds look.

BARAKA BOUTIQUE – SHOPFRONT HOME OF FORTUNE

above :: A ground-floor window framed in carved wood with protective iron bars is not uncommon in market homes, which are more outward looking than Stone Houses.

above :: Coral rag walls and banana trees form an enclosed garden oasis. The cement floor is painted with a rich apricot patina often used on interior walls of Swahili houses.

above :: A simple rustic door lacks the ornately carved center post and brass studs of the elaborate doors typical of Lamu's Stone Town and market area.

Looking for my mother's garden, I found my own.
— Alice Walker

above top :: The second-story courtyard leads to the sitting room that is located above the shop front, facing the street.
above lower :: Colonial-style furniture was favored by Indian merchants. Arab *dhow* sails inspired the lampshades.

above :: Shuttered windows set into a recessed arch look out across the street to the windows of another market house. The sill is decorated with tiles that were frequently used to decorate tables and chairs.

right :: On the rooftop, a cozy sitting area has been created with built-in stone benches like the Stone House *baraza*, here covered with cushions. The *makuti* (thatch) roof is typical of penthouse lounges.

*Our life's journey is an ever-unfolding work of
art that tells the story of where we have been
and with whom we have traveled.*
— *Iyanla Vanzant*

COLONIAL STYLE
HIJANI HOUSE

Acclaimed author Don Meredith and his editor wife Josie knew they had found their new home when they saw on the roof a *hijani* (ibis), the sacred bird associated with Thoth, the Egyptian god of arts and letters. Born and raised in California, the couple lived on a Dalmatian island as well as a Tuscan olive farm before coming to Lamu. They came to Lamu so Don could write *Where the Tigers Were: Travels through Literary Landscapes,* his prize-winning travelogue that follows the footsteps of expatriate authors from Karen Blixen to Graham Greene. The Merediths are well-traveled, intellectual, and hospitable—qualities also inherent in the Swahili values of *utamaduni* (cosmopolitanism), *ustaarabu* (world learning), and *ungwana* (integrity)—making Swahili *shule* a natural match for their artists' retreat. ***"It's a Trade Winds decor, a traveler's style that reflects personal journeys and spiritual pilgrimages,"*** Don explains. "That makes it very individualistic and, as a result, a style that works anywhere."

above :: Two chairs with seats woven in string show how local craftsmen adapt styles of European cane back chairs in Swahili culture. Midday sunlight filters through long, shuttered windows typical of storefront homes.

right :: The crenellated rooftop suggests an Arab fort, but the stone benches are in keeping with Lamu's style.

above :: The kitchen connects to the adjacent dining area through a trifoliate arch often used in Swahili mosques. A collection of fine European plates in an antique china cabinet reflects the Swahili fondness for displaying porcelain imported from China.

left :: The front room of the house has been converted into a dining area that looks out onto the veranda. Modern art complements the distinctly Swahili patina of beautifully finished coral walls. A *baraza* (stone bench) has been incorporated into the layout of the room. The ceiling incorporates mangrove poles and rafters in traditional Swahili style.

above :: The Turkish coffeepot sits on a small wooden serving tray. Embellished with brass tacks, it is typical of Gujarat craftsmanship from India.

left :: Polished with wax to a warm, luminous sheen, the living room floor is covered with a collection of rugs from Afghanistan, Turkey, and Pakistan.

Live harmoniously together like the coffee that takes the shape of the cup.
— *Swahili proverb*

Adobe Inns

HAVENS OF PURITY - SHELA
ADOBE INNS

Shela is a small fishing village that has developed a cachet among discerning travelers who seek the delights of both its coral reef and its coral palaces. Connected to Lamu by a seawall, Shela's mellow lifestyle has inspired many to put down roots and set up holiday homes in this peaceful corner of the world. The Stone Houses of Shela feature a layout similar to those of Mkomani, but in contrast to Lamu, where the density of dwellings permits only vertical expansion, Shela has ample space for new houses commissioned by the latest arrivals from overseas.

A walk along the oceanfront that leads to Shela provides a lesson in how the Stone Houses are built. Lashed to the seawall are potbellied *dhows*. From their holds, bare-chested stevedores heave ashore what appear to be overstuffed flour sacks and giant sugar cubes sparkling in the sun. Closer inspection reveals that they are 40-pound bags of lime and six-by-ten-inch coral bricks. The bricks are chiseled from Lamu's quarries of terrestrial coral, and the lime, also made of coral, comes from nearby Pate Island.

The coral goods are loaded onto convoys of *punda* (donkeys) laden with double saddlebags. Other donkeys drag bundles of 10-foot mangrove poles lashed to their withers. Coral blocks, coral lime, and mangrove poles have been the building blocks of the Swahili Stone Towns for thousands of years.

Waiting for work, teenage *punda*-wranglers gather by the old mosque with its distinctive conical minaret. Just as the church spire denoted village status in medieval European towns, the minaret was emblematic of a Swahili city-state. The Islamic faith introduced by Arabs imposed few obligations on the Africans, but it did require that a mosque be built for Friday worship. In return, local people gained membership in the *umma* (Islamic community), which included the Arabs who controlled the Indian Ocean trading network.

With its wide sandy streets, big blue sky, and undulating palm trees, Shela induces an expansive feeling of relaxation. Barefoot Swahili women saunter along with their veils floating behind them. The sun kisses their exposed faces, and the wind caresses their bare arms. Children tumble in the sand while fishermen mend turquoise fishing nets on the shore.

Today, however, with a flood of foreigners arriving in Shela to savor its serenity, construction is booming in the village. The man in demand is not a fisherman but a *fundi*—a master craftsman.

The status of the *fundi* in Swahili society is superior to that of an architect in the West. A *fundi* is to a Stone House as an *imam* (religious leader) is to a mosque. His job requires grounding in the traditional arts and fluency in several languages. To interact with his foreign clients, a *fundi* must know the new *lingua franca* of his trade—English. To manage his laborers, he must speak Urdu, Malabar, or Hindu. He must also know classical Arabic because, like fortune, artistic skills are considered as *baraka* (a blessing from God), and their application is predicated upon devotion to the holy language of the Qur'an. The *fundi* must also be of impeccable moral character. Like the *imam*, whose upright character

is fundamental to his mosque, the master builder requires *ungwana* (integrity) to ensure a faultless foundation upon which to build a house.

In building the coral houses, the *fundi* consults no blueprint. It is the environment, not the client, that dictates the dimensions of the house. For example, to achieve the optimal proportion of strength and length, mangrove poles used for ceiling rafters and floor supports are uniformly cut about 10 feet long.

The other essential building component provided by nature is coral. Light and porous, it breathes like a living organism in the hot tropical air. Stone houses washed down in the morning function in the same way as the unfired clay pots used for storing drinking water—water sweats from the interior to the exterior where, exposed to the hot air, it evaporates and cools the chamber within.

The small fishing village of Shela is reached by following the seawall from Lamu over the causeway that connects the two islands. Donkeys carrying bundles of mangrove poles and sacks of coral bricks are wrangled by teenage boys who oversee the transportation of building materials needed for new Stone House construction. In both Lamu town and Shela, new houses are going up to meet the rising demand for holiday hideaways.

Two different types of coral are used in building a Stone House. Living shallow-water coral is soft and can be carved easily for decorative accents. When it dries, it is durable. However, it is used sparingly to conserve supplies. Terrestrial-fossil coral rock, on the other hand, is found abundantly below ground. It is hard and can be cut into blocks that are strong but light. Laid like bricks, these are bound together by a mortar of weathered or burnt coral and sand, creating thick walls that insulate the house against heat. The Swahili Stone Houses are, in fact, buildings of *adobe*, an Arabic word from ancient Egyptian meaning 'brick'.

Coral scrap from terrestrial beds is also used for construction. Stone House roofs and floors (and the walls of modest homes) are made of coral rubble and mortar supported on the mangrove poles. When these surfaces are sealed and set, the ceiling functions as a shallow arch, buttressed by the thick sidewalls of the narrow galleries.

A further use of coral is to manufacture the lime used for mortar as well as the whitewash and finishing coats. Both terrestrial and sea coral, as well as mollusk shells, are good sources of calcium carbonate. When the coral is placed in stacks of coconut trunks that are set ablaze, the heat converts the calcium carbonate to calcium oxide, or lime. Mixed predominantly with earth, water, or very fine sand, it forms, respectively, mortar for binding, whitewash for painting, or the finishing coat that gives walls a distinctive apricot patina.

Fossilized coral just below the shallow soil substrata is quarried to provide coral bricks for Stone Houses. More modest homes are built with coral rubble mixed with mortar. Walls are then covered with coral plaster and coral-lime whitewash. Fine carvings and niches on interior walls are a Swahili specialty.

A visit to a coral house in Shela begins with pushing open the heavy front door. As it closes with a soft thud, it hushes the din of the noisy street and gives the impression of entrance into a hallowed space. Arriving in a shady antechamber, the visitor rests on a regal chair and eases feet free from shoes. The cool water of a foot fountain soothes tired muscles and rinses dust from the street. The faint murmur of the fountain and the subtle fragrance released from floating frangipani blossoms relax the mind. As the soles of the feet makes contact with the cool waxed floor, the soul connects with the serene coral environment of the Stone House.

As one steps into the open courtyard, the infinite expanse of azure sky pulls the eye and the spirit upward. Proceeding into the galleries, the absence of doors eliminates obstacles, encouraging the flow of energy. After the bustle of the street, the inner rooms offer a reposeful and uplifting retreat.

The building material (mangrove poles) and the architectural function (shallow arch) of the ceiling dictate the narrow depth of the galleries. Windows are eschewed since they compromise privacy and diminish the strength and insulating capacity of the walls. This could result in a cheerless interior if not for the elegant embellishments of the rooms. Decorative doorway jambs and lintels originally carved from soft reef coral are now often made from wood painted in stripes of burgundy, black, and white. These accents are complemented by

ornate designs carved into layers of coral plaster applied in designated areas that become larger and more impressive as one penetrates deeper into the house.

In the first gallery the carvings consist of a narrow strip around the three entrances. In the second gallery there is a wide decorative panel around the heavy wooden door that leads to the third gallery. A single column of small niches border both sides of the door frame, and the back walls of the two sleeping alcoves are embellished with an elaborate frieze of carved coral surrounding a small niche.

These niches have a functional purpose—like popcorn ceilings, the niches have many indentations to absorb noise and, carefully proportioned to distort perspective, they give a perception of added space—but their overall effect is distinctly spiritual. Wall niches in the side alcoves of the front galleries each display a single treasure or candle. Reminiscent of a Japanese *tokodomo*, they inspire

Because Islam prohibits representative art, the Swahili have refined the art of stylized designs. The beautiful niche found in the Lamu Palace Hotel has a traditional turtle shape. Heavy mahogany furnishings are also intricately carved. The niches hold treasured objects as simple as a shell or as sumptuous as a silver pen-and-ink set.

peaceful contemplation and evoke the Sufi analogy of God as "the light of a lantern in a niche." In the master bedroom, a multiplicity of niches display family heirlooms from past generations symbolizing the family's lineage, while unfilled niches await the generations to come. This inner (ndani) chamber functions as a grotto of tranquility rooted in the strength and purity of the family.

These wall niches, called *zidaka*, are perhaps the most unique feature of Swahili shule. More than any other single element, they imbue the house with serenity, spirituality, and sensuality. They arouse an organic sense of beauty that transcends the geometric design. Perhaps this is why they play an important part in Swahili weddings. Against the backdrop of the *zidaka* in the master bedroom, the bride sits in a trancelike manner while women and family pay homage to her beauty, purity, and heritage.

Dressed with intricate coral plasterwork, the whitewashed walls also complement the look of the Swahili patricians in their lightly scented *kanzu* (robes) and beautifully embroidered *kofia* (skull-caps). Both the plaster facade of the Stone House and the pressed costume of the Swahili men are expressions of *usafi* (purity). This quality, along with *ushwari* (calm) and *heshima* (honor), is an essential element of *ungwana* (integrity). A *fundi*, himself the personification of such virtue, has the ability to instill all these elements into a Stone House and the life of its inhabitants by using organic materials, adhering to time-honored proportions, and adorning interior walls with spiritual coral carvings.

Your real home is within.
— Quincy Jones

THE SWAHILI SANCTUARY
JOHARI HOUSE

Two centuries ago, on the occasion of his daughter's wedding, a wealthy Swahili patrician built for his *johari* (little jewel) a Swahili sanctuary that now welcomes travelers seeking to experience the spirit of Swahili shule. Deep within the *ndani* (inner) room of the house are located exquisite Swahili *zidaka* so rich and relaxing that they seem to connect visitors with their own *ndani* (inner) self. A composition in white, which is the resolution of all colors and the universal representation of *usafi* (purity), the *zidaka* radiate an air of reverence. Displaying a collection of art in a series of niches or one treasured object in a single niche, they invite the observer to focus on timeless beauty, releasing stresses of daily life. Contemplation of the patterns of light, the shades of white, and variations of design encourages the observer to transcend the material world and experience the seamlessness of the present and eternity. **One zidaka and one soul is all it takes to create a Swahili meditation center.**

above and right :: The influx of out-of-towners who are renovating houses has spurred a revival of traditional plaster and carving techniques that were on the point of perishing. Keeping walls properly whitewashed and adorning them with *zidaka* was considered an act of purification by Swahili patricians. *Zidaka* also had a practical effect: their dappled surface absorbed sound, discouraging eavesdropping in adjoining galleries.

above :: The right wall separates the second gallery from the first, and the coral niches on the left surround the entrance to the third or inner gallery. Customarily symmetrical, the two facing alcoves have been modified by inserting a window where a second niche would normally be found in a traditional Swahili Stone House.

left :: The sleeping alcove of the *msana wa yuu* has been converted into a sitting area. An old-fashioned sleeping cot for a child acts as a coffee table under a star-shaped light that complements the outline of the wall niche.

Though we travel the world over, to find the beautiful,
we must carry it with us, or we find it not.
— Ralph Waldo Emerson

 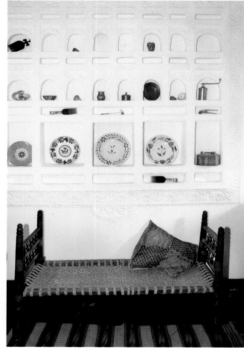 

above :: A traditional Swahili cradle features a *kikoi* sling suspended from a solid frame. This cradle is displayed in the Lamu Museum Stone House.

above :: In a neighboring home, a child's little cot is placed underneath the master bedroom's *zidaka* that displays antique ceramic plates and treasures from around the world.

above :: This elaborate cradle includes a canopy frame that would customarily be draped with a fine white voile to protect the infant from mosquitos and flies.

right :: A miniature four-poster bed with lace-bordered mosquito netting is so finely made that it appears to be a full-sized bed in a vaulted room.

We shape our buildings; thereafter they shape us.
— Winston Churchill

THE SHELA YOGA CENTER
FATUMA'S TOWER

Fatuma's Tower is a rambling coral compound built by antiques dealer and author Gillies Turle and his wife Fiammetta. A Tuscan native, Fiammetta studied yoga and meditation for many years in India before coming to Kenya to open her own yoga retreat. In Nairobi she met Gillies, who was writing *The Art of the Maasai* while managing Peter Beard's infamous *Hog Ranch*. In search of a place to house Gillies's antiques collection and Fiammetta's yoga practice, the couple came to Shela where they built a four-story villa, guest inn, and yoga center. Traditional Swahili techniques were used to create a Tuscan appearance, but the layout was also inspired by *vastu shastra* (house system), an Indian philosophy from the ancient Vedic culture from which yoga was developed. For example, as in Swahili Stone Houses, the adjoining **Yoga Retreat is built around an expansive central courtyard known in Sanskrit as brahmasthan, "the silent heart."** Like the *kiwanda* (courtyard) of the Swahili Stone House, it is grounded in daily activity, yet also connects the household to the heavens above.

above left and right :: At the entrance to the massage room, a colorful Indian cloth provides privacy while allowing circulation of cool breezes. A small foot fountain cleanses the feet and relaxes the mind with its fresh gurgling water.

right :: Soft light filters through netting into a serene guest bedroom in the guesthouse of the Yoga Retreat.

above :: A Swahili folding chair carved from a single piece of wood provides a surprisingly comfortable seat for reading or simply lounging.

above :: At the entrance to the study, a wall of white *zidaka* contrasts with the rich peach patina of the floor in the adjacent room.

above :: This beautiful example of a *kiti cha ezi* (seat of power) is made of ebony inlaid with mother-of-pearl and woven cane. Used ceremonially, it conveyed the high status of the owner or guest to whom it was offered.

left :: The living room of the Turles' private quarters features a deep built-in *baraza* covered with comfy cushions overlooking the thatched skyline of Shela.

above :: The interior of the shower is plastered with remnants of antique Chinese pottery that the owners uncovered on the site during construction.

above :: The arch of the doorway is mirrored by the arch of the window, which looks onto the sunlit *makuti* (thatch) roof of the Turles' private residence.

above :: Influenced by colonial Portuguese and Victorian British designs, tiles manufactured in India became popular replacements for Chinese ceramics. The blue flower is a symbol of the mystic center.

right :: On the rooftop, a semi-outdoor shower is housed within a cylindrical structure reminiscent of Shela's signature mosque minaret.

above :: An ethereal display of a creamy white *zidaka* highlights the spiritual ambience of the Yoga Retreat.

left :: The comfortable lounge of the Yoga Retreat looks out onto a sunlit courtyard called the "silent heart" by the ancient Vedic people who originated the practice of yoga.

Your real home is in your heart.

— *Iman*

above :: At the entrance to the walled compound, a corner *baraza* is nestled beside a coral rag wall in the shelter of a *makuti* (thatch) awning.

above :: The path to Shela's sand-dune beaches is approached through a whimsical wrought-iron gate inspired by children's stories written by the owner.

above :: Within the enclosed courtyard, three different types of coral finishes are shown on the *baraza*, the house exterior, and the compound wall.

right :: Within the central courtyard of the Yoga Retreat, glass buoys reflect the sunlight falling between dappled shade in a restful sculpture garden.

Restoration. I like the word.
The house, the land, perhaps ourselves.
But restored to what?
— Frances Mayes, Under the Tuscan Sun

STONE HOUSE SUAVE
CARLA'S HOUSE

"By living in a Stone House, I live a Swahili life— *relaxed and centered—*which is exactly what I need by the end of a school year," explains Carla Serantoni, a high-school teacher from Rome. Italians, she notes, have an obsession with decorating and embellishing their homes. But the Swahili style relies on the natural environment and spatial dimensions to provide a balance of the exterior and the interior, the public and the private. The minimal furnishings, uniform dimensions, and organic materials create a majesty that is the signature of the Stone House of the wealthy Swahili patricians. Like the shells that accessorize the interior, the house exhibits perfect symmetry and simplicity of form. *With a purity of intention, these Stone Houses of Shela relax the body and stretch time as effortlessly as do Shela's endless white beaches.*

above :: Glazed tiles inset into a side table complement the colors of handmade mats woven from doum palm. These tiles are used to decorate tables, benches, and headboards copied from Portuguese designs by Indian craftsmen.

right :: High four-poster beds made in Lamu have simple mattress supports of woven coconut coir. The feminine design of the Liberty fabric bedspread complements the ceiling's dark *boriti* (mangrove poles) and the burgundy, black, and white *banaa* (rectangular beams).

above :: Small niches in the coral plaster carvings that decorate a doorway are filled with objects of natural beauty from Shela's long, sandy beaches.

above :: A washstand showcases treasures found on the beach, including old Chinese plates that are often found buried beneath the sand.

above :: An unusual example of varnish embellishment frames a door. This work is typical of the neighboring island of Siyu in the Lamu archipelago.

I was not born for one corner;
the whole world is my native land.
— Lucius Annaeus Seneca

above :: The second gallery has been partially closed off by a wall of coral plaster that is dotted with small pieces of coral. In the background, the door to the *ndani* (inner) room that serves as a master bedroom is framed with coral carving.

right :: The beauty of this sleeping alcove relies entirely on the soft light and lofty height that provides a respite from the bustle of the outside world. Instilling a sense of calm and security is an important function of the traditional Swahili Stone House.

*If we are always arriving and departing,
it is also true that we are eternally anchored.
One's destination is never a place
but rather a new way of looking at things.*
— *Henry Miller*

A TRAVELER'S PARADISE
PEPONI HOTEL

Peponi Hotel is to Shela what Harry's Bar is to Venice. An entire enclave of expatriates, according to author John Heminway, "looks to Peponi as its watering hole, its nexus of entertainment, its fountain of gossip." A veteran of dozens of East African adventures, John maintains, **"Peponi is the resolution of all safaris in East Africa. It is the journey's exclamation point."** On the shores of the Indian Ocean, surrounded by fragrant frangipani and blossoming bougainvillea, Peponi lives up to its name, which means "a good place." But it is more than that. It's a longing that became a legend, a voyage that became a mooring, and a home that became a hotel. The Korstens, the sea-mad founders of Peponi, set sail from their cottage in Denmark over 40 years ago. By the time they reached Lamu, their teenage sons were in mutiny, desperate for the company of landlubbers. Today, the oldest son, Lars, and his English wife, Carol, run a tight ship in the Korsten family's *pied à sable*, which has been expanded into **one of the great little inns of the world.**

above :: The swinging beds of Peponi are adaptations of a style of outdoor porch divan that ensured wildlife wasn't found crawling into bed. Coconut coir rope is woven and lashed onto a simple wooden frame that supports a foam mattress for a relaxing seaside siesta.

right :: Breezes from the Indian Ocean blow through the sunroof penthouse suites, which are decorated in sunny yellow and rich earth tones.

above :: Plantation chairs with hinged arms that swing out were popular with British colonial officers who kicked off their riding boots, stretched out their legs on the extended arms, and sipped gin and tonic.

above :: Nestled in a blown-glass bowl from Nairobi, sweet-smelling frangipani flowers in the bedroom are a symbolic invitation to romance.

above :: As the sun rises, fishing boats set off from Peponi's pier, returning in the evening with the catch of the day for lucky diners.

Your happiness is my happiness.
— Swahili saying to a guest

above top :: Peponi is renowned for its excellent restaurant featuring fresh fruit from the sea and the land. At the request of guests, Swahili meals are served on brass trays and eaten with fingers by diners seated on the floor. Thick, strong, spiced coffee completes Swahili hospitality.

right :: Next to Peponi, cannons from an old fort guard the sea perimeter, watching over a steady flow of sailing *dhows*, fishing boats, and wind surfers that take advantage of the Trade Winds.

Honeymoon Hideaways - Island Atolls
Ocean Outposts

HONEYMOON HIDEAWAYS - ISLAND ATOLLS
OCEAN OUTPOSTS

A "sea-fari" is as essential to unveiling the Swahili Coast as a safari is to discovering the grassland savannahs. Sailing to the coral atolls that dot the coastline, the traveler discovers picturesque *shamba* (garden) villages of thatched cottages and thriving terraces under a canopy of massive mango trees and slender coconut palms bending in the humid Trade Winds.

These Shamba Villages evoke beach shack rather than city chic. Yet the Shamba Home is as quintessentially Swahili as the Stone House. While the Stone Town residents are traders and merchants, the village inhabitants are gardeners and fishermen. With their carefully tilled plots and fertile fishing grounds, the villages have a symbiotic relationship with the Stone Towns, whose deepwater harbors on a barren coast are suited for expanding trade networks but not for nourishing a burgeoning population.

Lacking the resources for elaborate Stone Houses, the villagers build homes from thatch, mangroves, and coral rock. The most rudimentary type of country home is little more than a cottage *(banda)* made of palm matting. More substantial homes are rectangular structures built on a framework of thin mangrove poles tied together with coir ropes. The poles support walls reinforced with red clay and lumps of coral limestone.

Between the houses are vegetable gardens for private consumption, along with family-owned trees. The most important is the coconut palm, grown for copra, coir, cooking oil, wood, building fronds, and matting. Fruit trees include mango, citrus, plantain, kapok, lychee, jackfruit, breadfruit, plum, and durian. Cash crops are grown in outlying community fields from which the bush has been cleared, revealing deep crevasses in the coral substrata. Filled with sifted soil, these crevasses nourish millet, maize, cassava, sweet potatoes, sesame, chilies, tomatoes, eggplants, and tobacco.

With its dirt streets, simple cottages, and lush vegetation, the village presents a very different picture from the cobbled passageways and whitewashed townhouses of the Stone Town. Chickens, geese, and goats cluck, cackle, and bleat; ox carts groan under loads of seaweed and thatch. Little boys race model *dhows* in the sea, while young

Along the coast and on coral atoll islands, shamba (garden) villages are home to farmers and fishermen who build small dwellings of coral rag cut from coral outcroppings and thatch woven from palm fronds. Complementing the vibrant colors of the Shamba Homes, women wear bright kangas (cotton sarongs) emblazoned with bold proverbs.

girls heft infants on their hips. Women wearing brightly colored *kangas* (sarongs) sing as they till the fields of crops and beds of seaweed. They spread their harvest from the land and sea on the ground, making patchworks of color: purple and magenta from algae and seaweed, sienna and umber from copra and coir, yellow and orange from rice and millet. Others sprawl with babies and neighbors on deep *barazas,* sifting grain, braiding coir, and embroidering caps.

In spite of their superficial differences, the Shamba Village adheres to many of the same concepts that underlie the Stone Town. Homes also employ the intimacy gradient, albeit a watered-down interpretation of it. As in the Stone House, the most public area of the Shamba Home is the front porch with its stone bench. This is often merged to form a deep recessed platform that provides convenient shade and space for communal activities or merchandise display. A modestly carved door, set back slightly from the street, provides entry to the family reception hall *(ukumbini),* a roofed room that takes the place of the Stone House courtyard. Often housing a trestle sewing machine, it is sparsely furnished with low cots, and the hard dirt floor is covered with brightly woven mats.

Like the Stone Town, each village has a mosque. It is so inconspicuous, however, that only an adjacent water well used for ablutions distinguishes it from the dwellings. Even in the simplest villages, men don clean, perfumed white robes and embroidered skull caps for evening and Friday prayers.

As residents gain wealth, they apply coral plaster to their mud and wattle homes. Front yards are swept immaculate every morning. These are expressions of *usafi* (purity), as important in rural villages as in urban centers. They identify a pious community in the midst of a profane wilderness.

This sacredness is preserved not only by experts steeped in the Qur'an but also by *waganga* (shamans) skilled in dealing with *pepo* (spirits), *shetani* (devils), and *mizimu* (ancestor spirits). This provides a spiritual complexity to Swahili religion and custom. For while the forefathers of the Stone Town patricians were Arab traders and scholars who observed *dini* (Muslim creed), the predecessors of the *shamba* folk were Bantu farmers and fishermen who brought *mila* (African traditions) into Swahili culture. This interesting duality is reflected in the Swahili belief in one God known by two names: *Allah* and *Mungu*.

The Bantu spread from their homelands near modern Cameroon and Nigeria at the beginning of the Christian era. They gradually engulfed indigenous groups speaking Khoisan languages, who may have been the first inhabitants of East Africa but who were disadvantaged by subequatorial Africa's lack of plants and animals suitable for domestication. The Bantu brought with them agricultural crops and cattle from their homelands north of the equator. They lost their cattle to disease-carrying tsetse flies in the Congo rainforest, but restocked from Nilo-Saharan and Afro-Asiatic herders who reached East Africa from the north. These groups also provided

the Bantu with crops such as sorghum and millet. Along the way, the Bantu also learned iron-smelting skills from African smiths who made steel in ultrahot furnaces 2,000 years before a similar furnace was invented by the British inventor, Sir Henry Bessemer, in the mid-19th century.

By the 1st or 2nd century AD, the Bantu farmers had advanced more than 2,000 miles to the eastern and southern coasts of Africa in one of the most impressive peaceful expansions known to scholars of prehistory. One area near Lamu in which they settled was called Shungwaya—the cradle of the Swahili people, according to legend. Shungwaya was ruled by a royal court consisting of the king, his courtiers, ministers, priests, and wizards. They believed in a plethora of spirits but had one paramount god who was the source for the moral code of *ungwana*, to which the Sungwaya elite were bound. Adherence to *ungwana*, loosely translated as "integrity" and consisting of noble virtues such as hospitality, honor, good manners, and proper grooming, became a key attribute of the Swahili character.

The chiefs of Shungwaya, revered for their magical powers, were impressed with the science, medicine, and astrology of their Arab trading partners. Inter-marriage with the Arabs and conversion to Islam added to their own spiritual and material power. As a result, *dini* (Muslim creed) supplemented, rather than replaced, the rituals and customs of Shungwaya. This is particularly true in the Shamba Villages, which remain a stronghold of *mila* tradition. For example, as in the Qur'an, *mila* contends

that the spirit world is as real as the human world. In every village, complementing the village mosque, there is a *mzumini* (spirit house), a scaled-down version of the thatch house where a variety of spirits are believed to dwell. Other spirits associated with nature live in caves and forests marked by a red, white, or black *shuka* (cloth) to signal the presence of saintly, fiendish, or demonic spirits respectively. Ancestor spirits are also venerated, including the "living dead"—deceased family members still present in memory.

While religious matters are dealt with by the *mwalimu* (Muslim teacher), spirit wrangling is handled by the *mganga* (shaman). In traditional Swahili thought, all human troubles are caused by envious spirits. Created by God as bodiless beings, capricious spirits consumed with jealousy over the corporeal bodies of humans will take possession of an unsuspecting victim who will experience symptoms such as poor health, mental conditions, relationship problems, and financial failure. Instead of exorcising the troublesome spirit, the *mganga* tames it in a ritual that lures the spirit out from the top of the patient's head.

In the modest country dwellings, bereft of *zidaka* with their spiritual effect, *mila* provides other ways to infuse a home with purity. Burned in chalices of hot embers, sweet-smelling incense gum eliminates odors thought to attract malevolent spirits. Amulets containing verses written in black-rice ink also help to keep spirits at bay.

The mganga (shaman) plays an important role in the Shamba Villages, regulating the antics of spirits that lurk in the dark and take forms such as owls. Spirit houses accommodate ancestor spirits that are invoked for community events such as planting fields or harvesting crops. Incense is one means of placating spirits and purifying homes.

Similarly, *mila* provides alternative ways for women to maintain personal *usafi* (purity). In the Shamba Village, as in other Bantu societies, women are indispensable to the local economy, so seclusion is neither economically possible nor culturally dictated. Manners defined by *ungwana* rather than the all-concealing black *buibui* provide appropriate ways to preserve honor in public spaces. In a society that prides itself on decorum and harmony, open confrontations are discouraged, so Swahili women have developed art forms that give voice to their emotions. They "talk back" with proverbs emblazoned on the back of the *kangas* they wear around their waists and heads. They lecture via symbolic representations of poetry woven into straw mats. They tease with hands painted with henna. They seduce with beds sprinkled with jasmine buds. These are ways to preserve purity, demonstrate respect, and maintain an intimacy gradient while asserting personal feelings.

In a society devoted to the belles-lettres, female poets and singers also used complex rhyming and witty double entendre to vocalize personal feelings. Their proverbs, poetry and lyrics became as important in Swahili vernacular as Aesop, Shakespeare, and the Beatles are in the English language.

To the uninformed observer, the Shamba Home may appear the opposite of the Stone House, but upon reflection it is clear that both uphold the values of Swahili *shule*. Only by unraveling the ways that Swahili beliefs have been applied in the countryside towns and ocean outposts can it be understood that Swahili *shule* is as pertinent to the Shamba Village as it is to the Stone Town.

No man is an island.
     — John Donne

Shamba Charm
Manda Bay

East Africa's romantic honeymoon hideaways on coral atoll islands evoke the spirit and charm of the homes in the Swahili *shamba* (countryside). The beachfront bungalows of Manda Bay are constructed of coral adobe with *makuti* (palm-thatch) roofs, much like the *banda* cottages of the Swahili villagers. In the *shamba*, each family has its own garden plot and fishing ground and also participates in tending community fields. At Manda Bay, each guest enjoys a private grove of coconut trees and a white sandy beach and joins in group activities like dining and diving. A perfect location to recharge the spirit and the soul, these coral atolls act like the coral *zidaka* (carved niches) of the Stone House, conveying what T. S. Elliot called ***"the still point of the turning world."*** Although distinct from the Stone Houses, the Shamba Home also is a sanctuary of simplicity, spirituality, and sensuality that is inherently African and distinctly Swahili.

above :: Walls made of coral rag are characteristic of Shamba Homes. A deep overhanging roof of *makuti* (palm thatch) supported by a frame of mangrove poles provides a shady perimeter to the house.

right :: A plain mat is covered with another colored with natural dyes, exemplifying the different types of matting that cover the floors of Shamba Homes.

above :: A Somalian *kikoi* woven with gold threads combines well with beaded sandals made by Swahili artisans.

above :: An old sailing *dhow* is beautifully decorated with carved panels gaily painted in blue and white.

above :: New *dhows* are still being built by hand in the boat yards of the Swahili coast. Small *dhows* like this one are used for fishing.

We are all islands in a common sea.
— Anne Morrow Lindbergh

above :: The crystal clear waters of the Lamu archipelago are home to a tremendous variety of tropical fish and coral species. The coral reef is one of the world's most diverse ecosystems, surpassed only by the tropical rainforest. Yet it is often overlooked by tourists who associate East Africa with the Big Five—elephant, water buffalo, lion, leopard, and rhinoceros.

Do not set sail using someone else's star.
  — *Kanga proverb*

SHAMBA SPIRIT
KIWAYU

Kiwayu is situated on a deserted beach in the northern Lamu archipelago. Its hallmark is the *kanga*, the bright cotton cloth worn in pairs around the waist and over the head of *shamba* women. Dried in the sun, stored with jasmine sachets, and scented with incense, the *kanga* contributes to the owner's *usafi* (purity). Swahili women, who pride themselves on composure and decorum, use these textiles to give voice to powerful emotions while avoiding direct confrontation—woven into each vivid cloth is a Swahili proverb. ***Like a romantic or tactful greeting card, suggestive and obliquely worded kanga are given by men to their sweethearts,*** by women to their rivals, by daughters-in-law to their mothers-in-law, or by girls to their friends. At Kiwayu, the predictable bathrobe is substituted by a *kanga* folded over the bed that welcomes each guest with a proverb such as ***"Mgeni njoo mwenyeji apone."*** **(Let the guest come so that the host is blessed.)**

above and right :: The main *banda* looks out over the Indian Ocean to the surf breaking on the reef and beyond, to the mainland of Kenya. In a guest *banda*, the azure color of the sea is repeated in the curtains and tablecloth. Beckoning guests to partake in a Swahili siesta, a hammock is filled with overstuffed pillows covered in the brightly printed *kangas* worn by *shamba* women.

above and left :: Worn in pairs, with one wrapped around the waist and the other cascading over the head and shoulders, *kangas* are the twin-sets of Swahili couture. They have bold designs illustrating a proverb printed at the bottom of each panel. Their bright graphic designs make them suitable for a variety of uses, such as pillow covers in Kiwayu's main lodge.

Be of good behavior with a discreet tongue so that you may be as one beloved wherever you enter.
— Mwana Kupona, Lamu poetess

above and right :: The saturated colors of the *shamba* women's *kangas* complement the technicolor hues of the Indian Ocean's tropical fish. Above ground, the terrestrial coral is as black and sharp as volcanic lava; underwater species of fish are iridescent shades of purple, orange, gold, and green.

The whole world is moved forward by good character;
The most wonderful thing is a wise character.
— Shaaban Roberts, Swahili poet

SHAMBA CHIC

MNEMBA ISLAND LODGE

Off the coast of Zanzibar, **Mnemba is a world-class retreat frequented by discerning travelers, among them Bill and Melinda Gates and Naomi Campbell.** It features cottages made of *makuti* (palm thatch), the same material used to build simple *shamba* dwellings. Framing the windows are sections of colorful floor mats that contain symbolic messages silently expressing the private sentiments of the weaver. Just as there is an inner *(msana cha ndani)* room in the Stone House, there is an inner language *(kiSwahili cha ndani)* of literary allusions and symbolic designs in this society devoted to belles lettres. Swahili women, in particular, are accomplished poetesses of both epic poems and pithy proverbs so popular that one word conveys a complete quote. A mat woven with a border of plump mango silhouettes brings to mind the proverb, "A ripe mango has to be eaten slowly." The wife places the mat by the matrimonial bed to remind her eager husband that appetites are best satisfied with leisure and care.

above and right :: The main *banda* (cottage) on the edge of the sea provides a shady retreat from the hot equatorial sun. Mat blinds can be rolled down on windy days. Plump pillows are covered with fabric made from locally grown hemp.

Mnemba Island Lodge – Shamba Chic

above :: A spacious bed is tented with sheer netting to create a romantic room-within-a-*banda*.

left :: The window frame and railing of the hut are bordered with matting made from strips of doum palm that have been naturally dyed.

above :: *Kikoi*, the traditional striped cotton sarongs used by fishermen or worn under a patrician's *kanzu* (robe) are ideal for resort beach wear.

above :: On these idyllic coral atolls, while visitors luxuriate in romance, Swahili women weave symbols of love and prosperity into the designs of mats. These are used for flooring in Shamba Homes and sometimes, as in Mnemba, to construct simple dwellings.

The beginning of mat-making is two slips of raffia.
— Swahili proverb

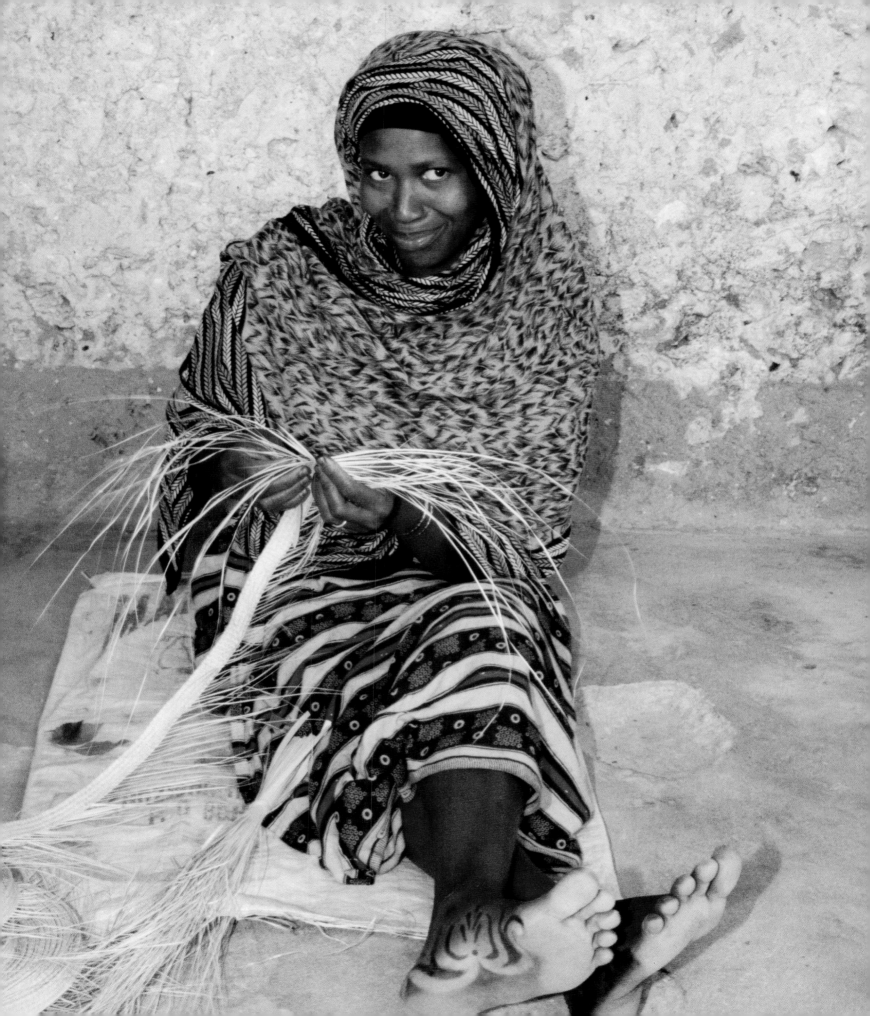

TROPICAL RETREATS - MOMBASA & MALINDI

BEACH & BREAKFAST

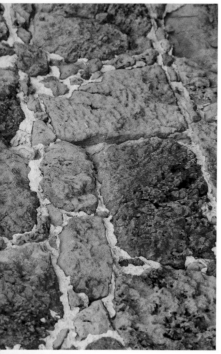

TROPICAL RETREATS - MOMBASA & MALINDI
BEACH & BREAKFAST

"Completely unmatched in the world," Ernest Hemingway wrote of Mombasa and Malindi. Lapped by turquoise waters, the coast is fringed with coconut palms and scrub pine, scented with frangipani and jasmine, and serenaded with bird song and monkey calls. Technicolor fish shimmer among the coral reefs where reef-building corals compete as the coast's most brilliant architects. Once Mombasa and Malindi represented the best Swahili Stone Towns, but, pillaged by invaders, they remain mere shadows of their previous splendor. More telling are the architecture and interiors of new resorts and vacation homes that illustrate elements of the coast's storied past.

These shores have attracted treasure seekers and holiday makers for thousands of years. Gedi, Kenya's oldest ruin, was a beach resort for elite Swahili in the 9th century. Today, the coast is a playground for Europeans, Asians, and North Americans. Outsiders once sought gold ingots and ivory tusks; now they come for golden sunshine and white sand beaches. A product of many cultures, Swahili shule can only be understood by taking into account the waves of foreigners that have swept into these port towns.

Among the first to land were *waq waq*, Indonesians named after the outrigger canoes that brought them 3,500 miles to East Africa. They arrived literally hungering for local culture; they were cannibals, according to many accounts. Chased off to Madagascar, they left a cultural imprint in the slender outrigger canoes that skim the waves, and the bright xylophone notes that ring in Swahili tunes. The crops they brought from Asia—bananas, yams, sugar cane, breadfruit, mangoes, lentils, and spices—became staples throughout Africa.

On their ocean crossing, the Indonesians encountered the "sewn boats" of the Arab traders, mentioned in the 1st-century nautical guide, *Periplus of the Erythraean Sea*. These boats had sails of palm matting and hulls made of wooden planks lashed together with coconut-fiber cord. Arab legends such as Sinbad the Sailor maintained that this prevented the vessels from being torn asunder by the treacherous Magnetic Mountain, claimed

Mombasa and Malindi have for millennia been critical hubs of the Indian Ocean trade network. Mombasa is now Kenya's busiest port and Malindi is a favored beach resort for European tourists. Once famous for their Stone Towns, which were sadly damaged by Portuguese invaders, they now display a range of architectural styles reflecting the many cultural influences in Swahili history.

to suck nails from ships that came near. The less sensational truth was that Arab shipbuilders lacked iron for nails. More importantly, they wanted to discourage others from discovering the secret of the monsoon winds that linked the markets of the Far East with those of Arabia and East Africa.

Each leg of the journey took many months, leaving little time for local trading. This was left to Swahili middlemen who ferried merchandise up and down the coast. By taking part in the Trade Winds network, the Swahili tapped into the exchange of luxuries originating in far-off lands from Shiraz to Shanghai. Persian rugs, Chinese porcelain, Iraqi lamps, Indian silks, Ceylonese jewels, Turkish rugs, and Venetian glass were commonplace in the well-appointed homes of the Swahili patricians.

By AD 1071, Swahili emissaries were voyaging as far as the royal courts of China. Two hundred years later, the first Chinese arrived in East Africa. They sought riches, especially ambergris, which was as valuable as gold. But they were also drawn by the coast's reputation for magic, for which Malindi in particular was known. A giraffe sent to the Chinese emperor from Malindi was believed to be a *quinlin*, a mythical animal bringing peace and prosperity.

In the 15th century, the Ming Dynasty embarked on a naval campaign to bring East Africa and other distant lands under the umbrella of the Middle Kingdom. The compass, invented by the Chinese for feng shui, was used to set a course for 317 ships and 27,870 men dispatched in seven expeditions led by Star Rafts. These were ships four times the

size of Columbus's *Santa Maria*, or nearly twice the length of a football field. They carried four years' worth of supplies along with treasures intended to win the hearts of people in distant lands.

The Columbus of this expedition was Grand Admiral Zheng. A Muslim captured from Mongol tribes, he became a royal page and was, accordingly, castrated and renamed Three Jewel Eunuch (from the Buddhist phrase "the three jewels of pious ejaculation"). Fluent in Mandarin and Arabic and accompanied by translators, scribes, scientists, doctors, and biologists, he spearheaded Chinese explorations in East Africa, Australia, and perhaps even the Americas. But following the emperor's death, Confucian bureaucrats disbanded the outward-looking Muslim eunuchs and redirected Chinese energies inward.

As China retreated, Portugal prepared. The Portuguese had seen the riches of the East in the conquered city of Ceuta and had learned from prisoners of war about camel caravans that journeyed across the Sahara to a "river of gold." But with no Mediterranean coastline, they were cut off from ships from Venice, who had a trade treaty with the Turkish Ottoman empire that controlled the ports where the goods arrived. The only way Portugal could break the monopoly was to circumnavigate Africa. They sent spies, Arabic-speaking Italians and Jews disguised as Muslim merchants, who returned with maps and marine innovations such as the triangular Arab lanteen sail (from the word *Latin*) seen in Italy. They conducted secret exploratory voyages until

Fort Jesus was built of coral by carpenters, stone masons, and laborers from the Portuguese colony of Goa at a time when the Swahili had been decimated. Its indestructible twelve-foot-thick walls, crimson as if stained with blood, still stand guard over the crowded streets of Mombasa's Stone Town. In contrast, the ancient ruins of the Swahili city Gedi are lush, overgrown, and deserted.

the pope "divided the world" between Spain and Portugal with the Treaty of Tordesillas in 1494.

Finally, in 1497, the coast was clear for Vasco da Gama to set sail in two *naus* (gunboats) to India, but the course was unknown. The turning point of his mission was Malindi. Da Gama had antagonized the Sultan of Mombasa, who discovered that the foreigners posing as friendly Muslims were, in fact, Christians determined to control the spice trade. But the Sultan of Malindi, a fierce rival of Mombasa, embraced the Portuguese and provided them with the pilot who changed the course of Swahili history.

Guided by Ahmad bin Majid, one of the most skilled Trade Winds navigators, the Portuguese swiftly arrived in India. By the end of the century, King Manuel proclaimed the Swahili coast to be Portuguese territory.

Waiting in the wings were the Turks. The Ottoman Empire that ruled Egypt and Arabia was desperate to regain its monopoly of the spice trade. A Turkish buccaneer, Amir Ali Bey, came to the aid of the Swahili with ships and soldiers from the Somalis, who were equally motivated to eliminate the Portuguese from the coast.

Unexpectedly, the allied forces were upstaged by another player. The Zimba were a gang of desperate renegades driven north from their Zambezi homelands by the Portuguese. Their name, from the Swahili word for lion, suggested their ferocity and cannibalistic reputation. Zimba raiders had already consumed Kilwa, which was served up by a traitor revealing the hidden causeway and who was then, himself, eaten. The Zimba then moved on to confront the Turks in Mombasa. On their heels 19 Portuguese naval gunners arrived from Goa. Together they demolished the Turks. The Portuguese plundered Mombasa, and the leftovers went to the Zimba as their just desserts.

From the ruins of Mombasa's demolished Stone Town, the Portuguese built Fort Jesus, designed by a top Italian military architect. They shipped the seven-year-old heir to the throne, Yusuf, to Goa where he was baptized as Jeronimo, educated by Franciscan monks, trained in the colonial navy, and sent back as a Portuguese puppet. But it was not Dom Jeronimo who was to dominate this era of Swahili history. With a dramatic change of costume, he announced a new act. Dressed in a Swahili *kanzu* and brandishing a curved *khanjar* (dagger) dripping with the blood of the Portuguese

The back streets of Mombasa and Malindi bustle with the business of building furniture, producing accessories, and transporting goods for the popular resorts, travelers' inns, and vacation villas that cater to the coast's latest wave of foreign arrivals.

captain, Sultan Yusuf bin Hasan, a born-again Muslim, strode onto the stage.

This time the reinforcements from Goa were powerless—the architect had designed a fort so impenetrable even the Portuguese couldn't blow it apart. The armada sailed back home, leaving two ships to maintain a blockade. Yusuf captured the ships and fled the scene to join the company of English and Dutch pirates who cruised the tropical seas from Madagascar to Arabia. His naval training served him well—though he was always welcomed into Swahili settlements, for the rest of his life he warded off the Portuguese.

Meanwhile, another wave was building in the Indian Ocean. In 1696 the Sultan of Oman sent a flotilla of ships to finish off Fort Jesus and, after a 3-year siege, Oman took control of the Swahili coast. Slowly the Stone Towns demolished by the Portuguese were rebuilt.

While the architectural impact of the Omani sultanate is most lavishly expressed in Zanzibar, the contemporary inns and vacation villas of Mombasa and Malindi show the impact of Indonesian, Turkish, Portuguese, and Arab design. Incorporating not just East and West but also African and Arabian, Swahili shule may be the first *true* fusion style.

The world is a traveler's inn.
— Afghan proverb

TRUE WORLD FUSION
ALFAJIRI VILLAS

An hour south of Mombasa, three exquisite villas grace the secluded beach of Diani. Described by the British magazine *Harpers & Queen* as **"the most glamorous house on the Indian Ocean,"** the Cliff Villa features a horizon pool nestled on a small cliff lapped by ocean waves. Designed by Italian architect Armando Tanzini, who created many of Kenya's top boutique hotels and vacation villas, the Alfajiri Villas are owned by Dr. Fabrizio Molinaro and his wife Marika. A sought-after interior designer, she oversees their workshop, which builds furnishings for the villas and for their safari camp, Galdessa. The signature style of Alfajiri Villas combines high *makuti* roofs, ivory Danish floors, Lamu doors, Indonesian-inspired furniture, and artifacts collected from around the world. "The villas epitomize Swahili shule," Marika comments. **"It's a distillation of styles from the four corners of the world—African bush, Arabian caravanserai, Asian court, and European metropolis.** This is a style that will make any house look like the home of a world explorer or art collector."

above and right :: Plump chairs of petal-pink suede rest on sturdy squat feet of tropical hardwood in a living room that combines animal-print fabrics with sumptuous silk cushions. Mangrove poles have been used imaginatively to create a natural screen between the sophisticated interior and the wildly overgrown exterior.

Alfajiri Villas – True World Fusion

above and left :: An outdoor bed swathed in mosquito netting is a seductive throwback to the owners' safari background. The Indonesian design hints at the Pacific voyagers who, centuries ago, arrived on these Swahili shores.

Treat the world well. It was not given to you by your parents:
It was lent to you by your children.
— Kenyan proverb

right and above :: In the architect's private home, well-worn leather chairs and rich kilims give the room an air of masculinity, which is tempered by the ethereal feminine beauty of the coral carving around the doorway where geese insouciantly gather. A little girl's dreamy bedroom contrasts with a bachelor's divan.

Your house is the magnet of my feet when I walk,
and your person, the magnet of my heart and eye.
— Ahmed ibn Majid,
Trade Wind poet/navigator

ARABIAN CARAVANSERAI
INDIAN OCEAN LODGE

The Indian Ocean Lodge is an exotic caravanserai that reflects its historic setting. **The rounded minaret, arched doorway, and crenellated roof are reminiscent of the architecture of Malindi's Arab founders.** Whitewashed walls, mangrove rafters, and interior courtyards express the Swahili foundation, while lavish fabrics and furnishings from China, India, and Persia reveal the riches of the Trade Wind network. Penthouse verandas, looking out onto a turquoise sea reserve, lure visitors with a reputation for world-class, big-game fishing and scuba diving. When the tide is high, outrigger sail boats that hark back to Indonesian voyagers tack past the dock. Low tide exposes subterranean caves where crashing waves rumble with the refrain of the poet-navigator Ahmed ibn Majid's words. After being commanded to escort Vasco da Gama to India, ibn Majid wrote in his epic poem about the Portuguese conquest, "Oh, had I known the treacherous things they would do."

above and right :: The black-and-white striped canopy of the master bedroom suite mirrors the patterns of the black mangrove rafters on the white ceiling. In front of the bed is an antique Zanzibar chest studded with brass tacks, which was used by wealthy Swahili to store clothing. In the corner of the room, hidden behind drapes, are shelves for additional storage.

Indian Ocean Lodge – Arabian Caravanserai

above and left :: A cusped arch complements the shape of the window that looks out onto the interior courtyard.

above :: A fisherman's *kikoi* (sarong), woven in striking colors with silver threads, is a handsome fabric for seat cushions.

above :: The clean geometric lines of a window shutter highlight the majestic black-and-white theme of an Arab palace.

To get lost is to find the way.
— *Kanga proverb*

above and right :: Veranda chairs on the crenellated rooftop, typical of Arab forts, look down on the shoreline where Vasco da Gama first landed in Malindi. Malindi's ruler provided the Portuguese with the area's most experienced navigator to take them to India.

Which epochs are so hospitable as this
Indeed epochs do endlessly recur.
Only good ones last, in memory they remain!
— Taarab lyric

THE TRADE WIND STYLE
SERENA HOTEL

Set back from the powder-white coral sands and shimmering waters of the Mombasa National Marine Park, the **Serena Hotel is styled to resemble a 13th-century Swahili town complete with winding paths, carved balconies, and cool courtyards.** The interior décor blends time-honored Swahili carving with the jeweled glow of Arabian lanterns and the lotus cool of a Persian water garden. Evoking visions of Constantinople in the Middle Ages, the vivid stained glass and lavish woven fabrics hint at the colorful relationship that existed with the Turkish Ottoman Empire, who came to the rescue of the Swahili. The lucrative spice trade has given way to a flourishing tourist business drawn to Mombasa's high-action water sports, sybaritic sun worship, and edgy nightlife. In the city's swank nightclubs, Swahili bands blend sounds of the past—African drums, Indonesian xylophones, Arabian lutes, Indian harmoniums, Turkish flutes, and Portuguese ukuleles with traditional *taarab* (folkloric music) lyrics and modern rap music.

above and right :: A majestic four-poster bed is draped in seductive voile. The deep maroons and golden yellows of the room's fabrics accentuate the brass detailing of the lamp fixtures and the Zanzibar chest. White plaster carving completes the look.

above and left :: A kaleidoscope of colors brings to mind the luxurious interiors of Constantinople, the capital of the Turkish Ottoman Republic and home of Ali Bey, the buccaneer who came to the rescue of the Swahili in their battle against the Portuguese invaders.

above and right :: A water garden, formed by tiers of urns similar to those used to store oil, is a calm oasis. A reflection pool surrounded by tall coconut palms faces the azure sea.

above :: The design of Serena's beach restaurant is inspired by local *dhows*. An old glass buoy hangs from the upper balcony.

above :: Decorating the sides of the restaurant are *dhow* eyes, customarily used on the sailing boats to ward off the evil eye.

above :: An attractive brass door knocker is shaped like a boat's anchor.

*[Good character] is not the face or good appearance
or to be an exalted person with approved ancestors;
The real proof of character is intelligence.*
— Siti binti Saad, Taarab singer

*It was a full moon while I was down at Takaungu,
and the beauty of the radiant, still nights was so perfect
that the heart bent under it.
— Isak Dinesen (Karen Blixen), Out of Africa*

"OUT OF AFRICA" COLONIAL
TAKAUNGU HOUSE

In Out of Africa, *Karen Blixen described Takaungu as being* "so perfect that the heart bent under it." It was here that, following her divorce from her wayward second cousin Baron Bror Blixen, the author rejoiced in trysts with her paramour, the white hunter Denys Finch Hatton, who had a beach cottage on a sisal farm overlooking the sea. Situated on the same cove is Takaungu House. The home of Philip and Charlotte Mason, it has been in their family since 1840 when Philip's grandfather, a contemporary of Blixen and Finch Hatton, came to Kenya as a British civil servant. The colonial style—with its burnished parquet floors, dark paneled walls, hand-hewn timbers, and creamy plaster—contrasts with the Swahili *shamba* style, expressed in the fisherman's *kikoi* (sarong) sewn into big comfy pillows spread over a *baraza* (stone bench) in a pool courtyard awash with bougainvillaea blossoms. This novel juxtaposition brings to mind the quote from the Roman geographer Pliny the Elder that inspired Blixen's title: **"Always something new, out of Africa."**

above and left :: An outdoor living area by the pool combines rustic Swahili furniture made of coconut wood with comfortable cushions made of local hemp cloth. Breeze blocks have been cleverly assembled to resemble *zidaka*. Side benches, covered in *kikoi* (fishermen sarongs), are inspired by Swahili *baraza*.

Takaungu House – "Out of Africa" Colonial

above and left :: The bathroom is simple, awash with romance and sensuality. The semicircular bathtub is accessorized with antique silver toiletries, ostrich eggs, and a green painted bowl.

If I know a song of Africa, of the giraffe and the African
new moon lying on her back, of the plows in the fields
and the sweaty faces of the coffee pickers,
does Africa know a song of me?
— Isak Dinesen (Karen Blixen), Out of Africa

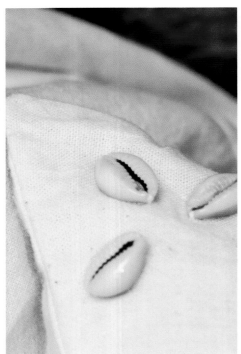 

above and right :: A pretty door carved with shell motifs provides a peek into one of several seductive guest rooms. Dark stained floors, fresh white linen, and corrugated tin roofs are reminiscent of the country homes of Karen Blixen, Denys Finch Hatton, and other legendary safari characters.

TAKAUNGU HOUSE – "OUT OF AFRICA" COLONIAL

above and left :: The living-room furniture is draped with heavy natural cotton fabric for an easy beach-themed lifestyle. The family dog keeps an eye on the property. In the study, a voile drape dances in the breeze of the Trade Winds.

above :: Sunset and sunrise mark the pace of an unhurried lifestyle in this beachside haven where the simple pleasures of life—fresh fruit, homemade delicacies, and a secret tryst—have always been safely guarded.

*History, like beauty, depends largely on the beholder.
So, when you read that David Livingstone discovered Victoria Falls,
you might be forgiven for thinking that there was nobody around
the Falls until Livingstone arrived on the scene.*
— Desmond Tutu

A SEA-FARI ESCAPE
SAMAWATI HOUSE

**"A sea-fari is to the coast as a safari is to the bush,"
explains guide extraordinaire Tony Church.** In the Maasai Mara, he runs safaris on horseback through herds of zebra, giraffe, impala, and hartebeest, with an occasional lion lurking behind. After an adrenaline-packed week in the saddle, clients kick off their riding boots and don flippers to drift with shoals of zebra fish, parrot fish, yellow tang, needlefish, and the ubiquitous lion fish tagging along. At Tony's beach cottage they discover that the Bright Four Hundred are as awesome as the Big Five. "First trod by elephants, inland safari routes were trailblazed by the Swahili who, centuries later guided Stanley, Livingstone, and other European adventurers," Tony explains. "To claim to have seen East Africa without exploring the Swahili coast would be as misguided as crediting the Victorian explorers with the 'discovery' of Lake Victoria and the source of the Nile."

above and right :: The delicate detail of the sheer white gauze is paired with a robustly carved hardwood bed under a vaulted ceiling of mangrove poles and heavy beams.

above and left :: Indian daybeds convert a humble space into an open invitation to lounge the day away in shady comfort. One headboard is richly carved with a seat of tightly woven cord while the other is decorated with a variety of painted tiles.

above and right :: The beauty of this seaside home lies in the timeless activities of the adjacent fishing village. Work starts at dawn as fishermen set sail in fishing dhows while villagers set lobster traps and collect seaweed in baskets woven of palm fronds.

The great morning which is for all appears in the East.
Let its light reveal us to each other who walk on
the same path of pilgrimage.
— Rabindranath Tagore

THE SULTAN'S PALACES

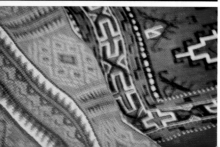

STONE VILLAS - ZANZIBAR
THE SULTAN'S PALACES

The Omanis called it *Zayn Zal Barr* (Fair Is the Island). This jewel of the Indian Ocean seduced the sultan of Oman with its deep harbors, fertile land, and wild game. Flush with their success in Mombasa, the Omanis proceeded to Zanzibar in the mid-19th century, where they toppled Swahili Queen Fatima and relocated their capital from the barren shores of Muscat to this lush green island.

Spanning the Gulf of Oman, the Indian Ocean, and the East African coast, the Omani sultanate became one of history's most notable non-European empires. It was also one of the important foreign influences that helped shape the development of a unique Swahili identity.

Like Mkomani in Lamu, the Stone Town in Zanzibar is a UNESCO World Heritage Site. However, it has a distinctive look that reflects Omani influence. Here the narrow alleyways are formed by freestanding coral mansions, their plain facades only occasionally lined with *baraza* (stone benches). Without the *daka* (porch), front doors open directly onto the street. The characteristic square-framed door of Lamu was embellished by Arab owners who added friezes engraved with Qur'anic inscriptions and by Indian merchants who capped their doors with arches carved with floral and animal designs. Huge brass bosses, strong chain locks, and heavy padlocks hint at the wealth within.

In place of the *daka,* a Zanzibar house has an Arab *majlis* (meeting room) on the ground floor at the front of the house. It has long shuttered windows looking out onto the street. Beyond are storerooms and a courtyard with a staircase leading up to the first floor. Another staircase continues up to the roof, which is crenellated like an Arab fort and peaked with a penthouse gazebo used as a tearoom. The traditional Swahili "intimacy gradient" that follows a horizontal north-south axis is thus converted here into what Zanzibar historian Abdul Sheriff calls a vertical "spiral of intimacy."

As in the Lamu Stone Houses, the two upper floors are the realm of the family, particularly of the women. But in the Zanzibar houses, the galleries, instead of being stacked one behind the other, are wrapped around the first floor courtyard. Doors lead into rooms with large windows that open to a view of adjacent buildings. The delicate *zidaka* (niches) of Lamu and Shela are replaced with large arched recesses used to display massive brass plates and other adornments.

In her autobiography, Princess Salome, the daughter of Sultan Seyyid, describes an elegant Zanzibar villa: "Persian carpets and fine mats cover the floor. Whitewashed walls are divided by matching deep recesses… from floor to ceiling… divided by [green] shelves. Upon these the choicest and most expensive objects… are symmetrically arranged… a handsomely cut glass, a beautifully painted plate, an elegant jug may cost any price: if it only looks pretty, it is sure to be purchased."

Between the recesses, the bare walls were almost completely covered with large mirrors from Europe, the occasional painting from Persia, and an abundance of wall clocks imported from America. The "gentlemen's room" was decorated with costly guns, daggers, and swords from Arabia, Persia, and Turkey. Tables were rarely used, but there were many different types of chairs. Clothes were stored inside numerous rosewood chests, beautifully carved and decorated with thousands of brass tacks.

In one corner of the room was a high double bed of carved rosewood with a canopy of white muslin or tulle. Princess Salome explains: "To get into them, one first mounts upon a chair or makes use of the natural step of a lady's maid. The lofty space under the bed is often used as sleeping space by others, for instance by small children's nurses or women attendants of sick people."

The Omani Arab household was as exotic as its furnishings. Muslim custom sanctioned four wives,

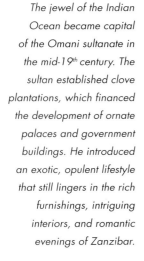

The jewel of the Indian Ocean became capital of the Omani sultanate in the mid-19ᵗʰ century. The sultan established clove plantations, which financed the development of ornate palaces and government buildings. He introduced an exotic, opulent lifestyle that still lingers in the rich furnishings, intriguing interiors, and romantic evenings of Zanzibar.

but rich Arabs enjoyed innumerable consorts. Sultan Seyyid set the standard: his harem in Zanzibar numbered approximately 100 concubines, each with her own eunuch, and in excess of 100 children. To keep jealousy at bay, the sultan followed a schedule of sleeping with five concubines each night in strict rotation (which meant, as one colonial administrator noted, that the most a concubine could look forward to was "a fifth of a sultan a fortnight"). Princess Salome describes the exotic intercourse of culture: "At least eight to ten shades of color could be found in the faces of the multitude… Persian, Turkish, Circassian, Swahili, Nubian, and Abyssinian were heard promiscuously next to Arabic, not to mention the various dialects of these languages."

Each group injected its own traditions of sensual beauty, making the Zanzibar harem a bed of riotous fashion flings. The subtle symbolism of the *shamba* styles erupted into an explosion of sexual innuendo. Bolstered with plump satin pillows and strewn with heady jasmine buds, beds stood in unabashed readiness, decorated with paintings of erect peacocks and redolent mangos. Women lolled in Persian baths, luxuriating in massages and spa treatments for hours at a time. Henna that traditionally colored only the tips of fingers and the soles of feet, imbuing a woman with *usafi* (purity), now spread over arms and legs in alluring patterns so seductive that its use was forbidden to unmarried women. Precious jewels, gold, and silver worn as nose rings, multiple earrings, layers of necklaces and pendants, rows of bracelets and ankle cuffs, and finger rings and toe rings consummated the new look. Values of *ushwari* (calm) and *usafi* (purity) were thus complemented by accents of sensual *uzuri* (beauty).

Sultan Seyyid was thus well accustomed to negotiating his way among cultural groups. Arriving on his first official visit to Zanzibar in his flagship, the *Liverpool*, which was accompanied by 100 *dhows* and 6,000 troops, Sultan Seyyid encountered Edmund Roberts, a New England captain from Portsmouth, New Hampshire. At the time, American ships—gunrunners and whalers—outnumbered the British, French, Dutch, and German ships in Swahili waters, which motivated President Andrew Jackson to authorize Roberts to negotiate a preferential trade agreement with the sultan. Zanzibar might have become America's most distant dominion if not for the inconvenient fact that the sultan was already bound by an identical agreement with the British. Forced to capitulate to the Americans, the sultan pledged the *Liverpool* to Britain's King William IV as a token of apology.

To build the new capital, Sultan Seyyid welcomed Indian merchants, giving them the same rights as his Arab and Swahili trading partners. He recruited thousands of Baluchi policemen from what is now Iran and Pakistan. Followers of the Aga Khan from Cutch and Kariawar prospered in commerce, while Bohara artisans and Afghani laborers built palaces, harems, and public baths. The Sinhalese focused on jewelry-making and the Chinese primarily harvested sea slugs and produced vermicelli.

The architecture of the Zanzibar seafront, with expanses of balconies looking out to the sea, has more in common with other Indian Ocean ports than with traditional Swahili Stone Towns. Omani influence is seen in the introduction of mosques with minarets and crenellated roofs, unlike the traditional Swahili mosque, which is barely distinguishable from a residential house.

In the wake of this rush to develop Zanzibar came the intrusion of European power. Sultan Seyyid had become rich by establishing clove plantations in Zanzibar. Slaves were made to work the labor-intensive crop and, as a result, Zanzibar became a slave market. All races and nationalities in the area were involved in this nefarious trade. Aroused by reports from the interior, which came from explorers Henry Stanley and David Livingstone—ironically led on safari by one of Zanzibar's principal slave traders—Britain imposed a treaty first limiting and then abolishing slavery. Sultan Seyyid, who had become dependent on British protection, had little choice but to accept.

After the sultan's death, a battle ensued between his sons for the throne. The new Sultan Majid banished his rival brother Barghash to India, where the exile was impressed by Bombay's urban renewal under British imperial rule. The new government buildings designed to legitimize the British presence blended Hindu, Mogul, and Islamic styles with European

Gothic to create Indo-Saracenic architecture. Upon his return as the new sultan, Barghash commissioned India's top architect to build palaces and ceremonial buildings in the same style, and wealthy Indian merchants followed suit. During Barghash's rule, Zanzibar emerged from the scramble for Africa as a British protectorate. The resident British architect appointed to build the concrete representations of the British Imperial Empire created Indo-Saracenic buildings that would look at home in Marrakesh, Istanbul, or even Disneyland. The result is a simple Swahili Stone Town surrounded by a showy array of resplendent domes, cathedral spires, castle turrets, and mosque minarets in a wild celebration of African, Arabian, Asian, and European styles.

Zanzibar gained its independence in 1963 and merged with Tanganyika the next year to form Tanzania. During the country's socialist period under Julius Nyerere, Zanzibar acquired several ignoble high-rise tenement buildings, paid for with Eastern-bloc assistance, in the outlying suburbs of

Zanzibar. A failing economy resulted in the slow demise of the Stone Town.

Now benefitting from a free-market economy, Zanzibar is working to preserve and revitalize Swahili culture. Its annual Festival of the Dhow Countries is a renowned international celebration of film, music, and art. A team of young cultural activists, both Swahili and international, work from headquarters in the Old Fort. Once Queen Fatima's palace and subsequently a Portuguese chapel, an Omani fortress, and a British tennis club, the Old Fort is a fitting site for a Swahili movement that draws strength from history to build new cultural ties. Activists trade e-mails with artists from Shanghai to Chicago, making use of both the traditional trade network linking the Indian Ocean region and the new information network uniting the global community.

New cultures and forms of artistic expression are received with typical Swahili hospitality. During festivals in the Old Fort, Swahili *taarab* bands and *ngoma* dance groups perform alongside reggae bands from Jamaica, rappers from Sudan, sufi dancers from Turkey, *capoeira* performers from Brazil, and gamelan orchestras from Indonesia. Bollywood extravaganzas screen as double features with Swahili soap operas and Swiss documentaries. Drawing on their past as commercial middlemen, the people of the Swahili coast continue to be cultural facilitators, adapting to new technologies and art forms and fostering a modern dialogue between cultures that lies at the heart of cosmopolitism and world learning.

Architecture is to make us know — and remember — who we are.
— Sir Geoffrey Jellicoe

THE CULTURAL JUBILEE
THE OLD DISPENSARY

The Old Dispensary exemplifies the Indian architectural influence in Zanzibar in the late 19th century. It was built by Tharia Topan, an Ismaili Indian merchant referred to as the Bismarck of the Swahili Empire because of his influence as an adviser to Sultan Barghash. Originally intended as a hospital to commemorate Queen Victoria's Golden Jubilee, the building has a grandiose architecture that betrays far larger designs. Its construction was a shrewd political statement at a pivotal moment in Zanzibar's history. Britain and Germany were jockeying for control of East Africa, with Zanzibar finally becoming a British protectorate. *The name—the Jubilee Hospital—professed loyalty to the British Crown, but the stained glass, colored to match the Ismaili flag, celebrated the power of the Indian community* in Zanzibar and the supremacy of Tharia Topan himself. Knighted by Queen Victoria, Tharia Topan died before completing his project. The building, eventually opened as a medical dispensary, was later restored by a foundation established by the Ismaili Aga Khan Foundation and now houses the Stone Town Cultural Center.

left and above :: The Dispensary is a very elaborate version of a veranda house. It was designed by Hasham Virjee Patel, the Indian architect responsible for the redesign of Bombay. Extending the full length of the building façade, two stories of balconies are supported by intricately carved brackets and delicate fascia boards.

Life is one long jubilee.

— Ira Gershwin

right and above :: Integrated into the Victorian embellishments is glazed colored glass in the red and green colors of the Ismaili flag. After Tharia Topan's death, the subsequent owners opened a medical dispensary on the ground floor and subdivided the upper floors into rental apartments. The building, restored to its original glory by the Aga Khan Cultural Services, once again dominates Zanzibar's seafront.

*I had been so happy at Bububu and could have had
no desire for anything better.*
— *Princess Salome, Memoirs of an Arabian Princess*

HAREM HIDEWAY
SALOME'S GARDEN

**The scene of passion, intrigue, and politics, this
mansion in the country village of Bububu was the
love nest of Bibi (princess) Salome in the 19ᵗʰ century.**
One of Sultan Seyyid's many children, she sided with
an older brother, Barghash, in his play for the throne
after the sultan's death. However, another brother
was crowned, and he exiled Barghash to Bombay.
He forgave Salome but neglected to find her a
husband. Taking affairs into her own hands, she set
her sights on a handsome German trader who she
saw across the rooftops. After trysts in Bububu led
to a pregnancy, Salome joined in the New Year's
rituals of bathing in the sea to wash away the
impuritites of the past year. She allowed herself to
be swept off by a sailor and boarded a Royal Navy
steamer bound for Aden. There Bibi Salome, an
unwed Muslim Zanzibar princess, was transformed
into Emily Ruete, a married Lutheran German *frau*.
Her autobiography, *Memoirs of an Arabian Princess
from Zanzibar*, documents her subsequent roles as
celebrated hostess, widowed mother, political spy,
and world-renowned author.

above and right :: The antique furnishings of Princess Salome's countryside palace transport the visitor to another age. The long, narrow rooms are given an illusion of space by tall shuttered windows accentuated with blue arches that look out onto the fruit orchard. A tiny sleeping alcove invites intimate pillow talk in this hideaway, rumored to have been the site of illicit trysts between the princess and her German lover.

above and left :: Decorated in soft peach and peacock green, Salome's bathroom invites long, sensual soaks in scented water. In her autobiography, the princess records her horror at discovering the bathing habits (or lack thereof) of 19th century Europe, which compared unfavorably to the lavish toilet of the harem ladies.

... the bath has been filled with fresh spring water,
and the garments ... strewn with jessamine and orange blossoms...
scented with amber and musk.
— Princess Salome, Memoirs of an Arabian Princess

above top :: Daily chores were performed on the front veranda to take advantage of the gentle winds. Cooking took place in an adjacent space with pots balanced on three rocks above hot embers. A Swahili proverb, "It takes three stones to balance a boiling pot," hints that it often takes more than a man and a wife to satisfy bubbling desires.

A good name shines in the dark.
— Swahili proverb

TOAST OF THE TOWN
EMERSON & GREEN HOTEL

This magnificent Stone House was once the home of Tharia Topan, the Indian merchant prince who, as adviser to Sultan Barghash, was intricately involved in the development of Zanzibar. Now it is a boutique hotel run by New York expatriate Emerson Skeens and his business partner Thomas Green. They were among the first foreign investors to come to the rescue of Zanzibar's Stone Town, which had been gravely neglected during Zanzibar's post-independence socialist experiment. *Now the toast of Zanzibar, the hotel is furnished like a Zanzibar harem, showing off the sensual and seductive side of Swahili shule.* Emerson, who is known locally as *Baba* (father), has also enhanced world awareness of Zanzibar by spearheading an annual international film and music festival—the Festival of the Dhow Countries. During the festival, Swahili artists mingle with artists and fans from as far away as China and Brazil in a celebration that exemplifies the Swahili ability to absorb the best of foreign cultures while preserving their own.

above and right :: Each room is a spare, yet rich, composite of robust antiques and refined fabrics, resulting in a daring, free-spirited interior that incites adventure and romance. Symbols of ripe readiness and flights of fancy are incorporated in the patterns of the tiles and the paintings on the headboards.

above and left :: A quintessentially Zanzibarian boudoir throbs with passion fired by jeweled rays of iridescent light created by panes of ruby red, emerald green, turquoise blue, and amethyst plum. The unbridled theatrical look reflects the owner's avocation—Broadway musicals—rather than his professional background as one of New York's top psychiatrists.

I'll come back to Zanzibar.
— *Billy Joel*

above and left :: The sumptuous Swahili bed is decorated with symbols of desire and lust—the proud, erect peacock and the flushed-pink blossom—and strewn with heady jasmine buds to invoke a night of passion and pleasure. In public, chastity rules; in private, carnal indulgence has free reign in seductive harem-inspired rooms.

right and above :: From the depths of the inn's lobby—dominated by a hedonic harem divan lifted straight from the last sultan's palace—to the rooftop restaurant, Emerson & Green exudes a spicy sensuality that scores top points with honey-mooners and lusty lovers.

It's not a loss for a bee to die for honey.
— Taarab lyric

It doesn't matter how long you forget,
Only how soon you remember!
— Buddha

HUES AND HARMONY
TEMBO HOTEL

Tembo is the Swahili word for elephant, the animal associated with memory. What do travelers most remember about the Tembo Hotel? Is it the striking black-and-white tiled floors that were inspired by the sultan's memories of his visit to Versailles? Or is it the white moldings around the high ceilings carved with geometric shapes to complement the creamy interior? Throw open the heavy wooden shutters and shafts of crimson, emerald, sapphire, and topaz light stream into the room, transforming the monochromatic interior into a Kodachrome print. Each pane of window glass is a different hue. Mixed together, they create all the colors of the rainbow. This vision reminds us that nothing is black and white. *Rather, it is the different filters through which we view life that color our perception of the world.*

above and right :: The rainbow of colors overlaying the black-and-white floor brings to mind the lyrics of the American song-writer, Joy Graysen: "Are you greater than the Sun that's shining down on everyone? Black, yellow, brown or red or white: don't we all deserve the Light?"

left and above:: In a guest bedroom, the bed is awash with light tinted from the colors of the glazed window that spills onto the white mosquito netting and the creamy interior walls creating a feeling of magical romance.

*May the Rainbow
Always touch your shoulder.
— Cherokee blessing*

above :: Tucked into every corner of the hotel are shuttered windows of saturated stained glass that open onto views of the beach below.

above :: A colorful doorway beckons guests to step out onto a generous verandah that faces the seafront.

above :: The open shutters of a cusped-arched window contrasting against the brilliant white wall create a distinctive look.

right :: The grand salon boasts an extravagant display of stained glass that frames the view of the Zanzibar harbor. Once crowded with Arab dhows, American whalers, and European steamers, the Zanzibar port is now the destination of cruise ships and dive boats.

Swahili Sanctuaries

AT HOME WITH SWAHILI

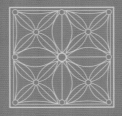

SWAHILI SANCTUARIES
AT HOME WITH SWAHILI

When I opened my traveling cases at home, the scent of the Swahili coast burst free like a genie set loose from a lantern. Gift packages of cloves, cardamom, and pepper had popped open. Henna had seeped out of the small hemp bags. Layers of *kangas* and *kikois* decompressed, releasing the smell of the fresh ocean breeze and sun-dried laundry. Unrolling a woven mat, I sensed coconut palm leaves mingled with the smoky hint of charcoal braziers.

From a material point of view, these trinkets had little value. But to me they were valuable souvenirs in the true sense of the French *se souvenir,* meaning "to remember." They would always remind me of my trip's most precious acquisition: the knowledge of Swahili shule.

I set off to East Africa in search of a style; I returned home to the West to apply it. Along the way I developed the notion of Swahili shule, a school of thought from the ancient Swahili civilization. In the Stone Towns and the Shamba Villages, I saw how the Swahili focus on *ushwari* (calm), *usafi* (purity), and *uzuri* (beauty) transforms a home into a sanctuary of simplicity, spirituality, and sensuality. Back home, I discovered that applying Swahili shule was fun and

easy. I sought out importers of Swahili furniture and tracked down lush fabrics. With *zidaka* replicas, I constructed my own Swahili meditation niche, and with colored film gels placed on window panes, I styled my own Zanzibar harem. I mounted a photographic exhibition and set up an online gallery at www.bibijordan.com. But as I created, I realized that Swahili shule is more than an architectural style or an interior-design philosophy. It is a way of thinking that offers lessons for achieving a life of tranquility and personal realization—lessons as relevant to our society as to the Swahili way of life 2,000 years ago.

In their homes and in their lives, the Swahili distinguished between the private and public spheres. Aspects of their homes and consciousness were allocated to public life, but ample space and consideration were reserved for nurturing the inner *(ndani)* self. Materially, this was represented by the beautiful *zidaka*, the unique Swahili meditation niches that invite contemplation on family heritage, purity, and the Infinite. Their noble code of ethics, *ungwana*, further encouraged personal comportment conducive to harmony, honor, and integrity. The public sphere extended from the local baraza

Western homes such as Bo van der Assum's upstate New York home (page 262 and 270–271) or Suad Cano's California townhouse (pages 264–267) successfullly integrate African and Arabian influences with Eastern and Western elements to create a sense of cosmopolitanism and world learning that is fundamental to Swahili shule.

to the far-flung lands of the Trade Winds network. Their cultural explorations were never limited by the boundaries of the Swahili city-states. The focus on *ustaarabu* (world learning) ensured a literate, outward-looking perspective linking them to cultures and bodies of knowledge that were foreign, but did not hold any of today's fear of foreignness. While they may not have agreed with all cultures, they comprehended the character of Africans, Asians, Arabs, and Europeans. In this way they exhibited *utamaduni* (cosmopolitanism) in the true sense of the word.

In the 21st century, for the Swahili as well as all of us, the public sphere has been extended by the web of communication technologies that encircles our globe. The Swahili survived clashes of cultures that were no less shocking than those we experience today. Yet through communication—verbal, cultural, and commercial—they initiated conversations between cultures that led to understanding and growth. Their model of a community built on *utamaduni* (cosmopolitanism), *ustaarabu* (world learning), and *ungwana* (integrity) provides a very relevant lesson for today's global community striving to create a world of balance and respect.

The last destination isn't the final place on the itinerary,
but what happens when we return home and try to make sense of it.
— Pico Ayer

SWAHILI SANCTUARIES
SWAHILI SHULE IN AMERICA

In three different houses, three designers illustrate how Swahili shule can be incorporated into Western homes. In his traditional home in the verdant countryside of the Catskill mountains, Bo van der Assum uses mahogany tables from Lamu Industries to add a stately masculine touch to airy conservatory rooms (pages 262 and 270–271). In her contemporary townhouse on California's Santa Monica beachfront, Suad Cano blends Swahili doors with Middle Eastern fabrics, Asian art and European furniture to create a Trade Wind home (pages 264–267). In a 1950's bungalow in Los Angeles' San Fernando Valley, Lea Keyes fashioned makeovers inspired by Swahili shule (pages 268–269 and 272–274). In each home, the fusion of Africa and Arabia with East and West reminds us of our global tribe's interconnection of all cultures. As the Swahili Sufi mystics taught: ***Each culture explored is like a new facet carved into a diamond, conducting light into the center and radiating outwards all the colors of the rainbow. The diamond is Self and the rainbow is Humanity.***

above and right :: An outdoor seating area reminiscent of Samawati House has been recreated in Los Angeles under a canopy of bougainvillea blossoms with a Swahili-style wooden bench inlaid with painted tiles purchased from Berbere Imports in Los Angeles. These benches, as well as side tables, are becoming increasingly popular with home furnishing importers appealing to customers looking for a touch of the exotic in their interiors.

Within the image: CAMP RIP VAN WINKLE

above and left :: A classic American home in the East coast countryside showcases a variety of mahogany tables made by Lamu Industries that are marketed by *www.lamu.com*. Their sturdy dark tropical woods contrast with the honey-stained oak floors. African fabrics and Swahili *kikois* cover oversized sofas.

Each day is a journey and the journey itself home.
— Basho, Japanese poet

above and right :: A seductive plein air harem tea party relies on an unconventional blend of fine European antiques, bold Middle Eastern cushions, and a rich Indian sari tablecloth accessorized with lanterns, plates and votive candle holders widely available in retail shops.

above and right :: Inspired by Zanzibar's Emerson and Green, British designer Lea Keyes transformed an ordinary mono-chrome bedroom in California's San Fernando Valley into a rainbow of romance. A canopy frame attached to the ceiling and draped with dreamy voile envelopes a simple bed in an air of feminine seduction. Film gels cut to fit the panes of an easterly window fill the room with shafts of jeweled light.

above and right :: The same bedroom was transformed into a harem boudoir by replacing netting with an assortment of rich silk fabrics and golden tassels. A Balinese doorframe placed at the head of the bed invokes memoirs of the intricate latticework that shielded the Sultan's harem from the public. Colored gels placed over the glass of an Indian lantern complete the look of opulence.

You have no idea of what is in store for you,
but you will, if you are wise and know the art of travel,
let yourself go on the stream of the unknown.
— Freya Stark, Baghdad Sketches

We don't receive wisdom;
We must discover it for ourselves after a journey
that no one can take for us or spare us.
— Marcel Proust

SWAHILI GLOSSARY

Note: Swahili grammar differs markedly from English. The plural is formed not by adding a suffix such as 's' but rather by changing the prefix. However there are 7 different categories of nouns each using a specific prefix to form the plural. To simplify this, Swahili words used in the text have been largely limited to the singular.

Ajaib	wonder	*Kikoi*	stripped cotton sarong
Babu, pl. mababu	grandfather	*Khanga, pl. khanga*	women's matching cotton wrap
Banaa	squared mangrove roof joists	*Khanjar*	curved dagger
Banda, pl. vibanda	cottage, hut	*Kidara cha meko*	rooftop kitchen
Baraka	blessing	*Kiswahili*	Swahili language
Baraza	stone bench	*Kitanda, pl. vitanda*	bed
Bibi, pl. mabibi	wife, princess, grandmother	*Kiti, pl. viti*	chair
Boriti	rounded mangrove roof joists	*Kiwanda, pl. viwanda*	courtyard
Beit	house	*Kofia, pl. kofia*	men's embroidered skull cap
Buibui	women's black over-gown	*Majlis*	meeting room
Choo, pl. vyo	bathroom	*Makuti*	thatch
Daka, pl. madaka	porch	*Mbambakofi*	hardwood like mahogany
Dawa	herbal medicine	*Mganga, pl. waganga*	healer, shaman
Dhow	boat	*Mila*	traditional Bantu customs
Dini	Muslim creed	*Mkeka, pl. mideka*	woven mat
Fundi, pl. mafundi	master of craft	*Mkubwa, pl. wakubwa*	senior or important (person)
Heshima	reputation, honor, respect	*Mpingo*	ebony
Hijani	ibis, sacred bird	*Msana, pl. misana*	gallery, narrow room
Jahazi	type of dhow, boat	*Mtaa, pl. mitaa*	quarter, neighborhood
Jinni, pl. majini	spirit, jinn	*Mwalimu*	Islamic teacher
Johari	jewel	*Mwandi*	curtain rail
Kanzu	men's white robe	*Mzee, pl. wazee*	elder
Karibu, pl. karibuni	welcome	*Mzimu, pl. mizimu*	ancestor spirit

Ndani, pl. ndani	inner (room)	*Shule*	school
Ndia kuu	main road	*Taarab*	popular form of music
Ngoma	drum	*Tekani*	inner porch
Ntaanyao	stool for accessing high bed	*Ukumbine*	reception hall
Pavilao	high pavilion bed	*Ngwana*	civility, integrity
Pepo, pl. pepo	spirit	*Usafi*	purity
Peponi	good place, Paradise	*Ushwari*	calm, serenity
Punda	donkey	*Ustaarabu*	world learning
Rohani, pl. marohani	type of spirit	*Utamaduni*	cosmopolitanism
Sebule	guest room	*Uzuri*	beauty
Shaitani, pl. mashaitani	evil spirit	*Waq waq*	outrigger sailing boats
Shamba, pl. mashamba	garden, countryside	*Zidaka, pl. vidaka*	wall alcove
Shuka	cloth, loin cloth	*Zipya*	square column

TRAVELER'S GUIDE

Safari coordinators:

Bibi Jordan
bibi@bibijordan.com
www.bibijordan.com

A website for travelers and collectors.

- Fine art photographic prints
- Photographic greeting cards
- Gifts from Swahili artisan collectives
- Swahili fabrics and zidaka
- Books and videos
- CDs and DVDs
- Destination resource list
- Safari guide recommendations
- Swahili shule blog

East Africa:
Nancy Galloway
nancy@bibijordan.com

Southern Africa:
Diana Smullens
info@hospitalityafrika.com
www.hospitalityafrika.com

Designer:

Linda Prescott
www.lindaprescottdesign.com

Accommodation: (in order of appearance]

Baytil Ajaib	baytil@eihr.com
Beith Mkubwa	bo@mahoganytables.com www.mahoganytables.com
The Pool House	lamuhomes@swiftkenya.com www.lamuhomes.com
Hijani House	hijani@bibijordan.com
Peponi Hotel	peponi@peponi-lamu.com
Johari House	earnshaw@swiftkenya.com
Carla's House	carladelamu@hotmail.com
Fatuma's Tower	www.fatumastower.com
Manda Bay	bookings@mandabay.com www.mandabay.com
Mnemba	usa@ccafrica.com www.mnemba-island.com
Kiwayu	kiwayu@kiwayu.com www.kiwayu.com
Alfajiri Villas	molinaro@africaonline.co.ke www.alfajirivillas.com
Indian Ocean	www.africanmeccasafaris.com
Serena Hotel	reservations@serenahotels.com www.serenahotels.com
Takaungu House	pembaafloat@zanlink.com www.pembaisland.co.tz
Samawati House	logonot@samawati.co.ke www.samawati.co.ke
Salome's Garden	info@houseofwonders.com www.salomes-garden.com
Emerson & Green	emerson-green@zitec.org www.emerson-green.com
Tembo Hotel	tembo@zitec.org www.tembohotel.com

Go in peace; May God give you grace;
May He reward you well; Life is a journey.
— Swahili farewell

BIBLIOGRAPHY

Allen, James de Vere, *Swahili Origins*. Athens, Ohio: Ohio University Press, 1993.

Appiah, Kwame Anthony. *Cosmopolitanism: Ethics in a World of Strangers*. New York, New York: W.W. Norton, 2006.

Bose, Sugata. *A Hundred Horizons: The Indian Ocean in the Age of Global Empire*. Cambridge, Massachusetts: Harvard University Press, 2006.

Caplan, Pat. *African Voices, African Lives: Personal Narratives from a Swahili Village*. London, England: Routledge, 1997.

Crowther, Geoff and Hugh Finlay. *Kenya*. Melbourne, Australia: Lonely Planet Publications, 1994.

Farsi, S. S., *Swahili Sayings*, East African Literature Bureau, Nairobi, 1958

Ghaidan, Usam. *Lamu: A Study of the Swahili Town*. Nairobi, Kenya: Kenya Literature Bureau, 1992.

bin Juma Bhalo, Ahmad Nassir. *Poems from Kenya*. Madison, Wisconsin: University of Wisconsin Press, 1966.

Hall, Richard Seymour. *Empires of the Monsoon: A History of the Indian Ocean and Its Invaders*. New York, New York: HarperCollins Publishers, 1998.

bin Ismail, Hasani. *The Medicine Man (Oxford Library of African Literature)*. Clarendon Press, 1968.

Khalid, Abdallah. *The Liberation of Swahili from European Appropriation (A Handbook for African Nation-Building, v.1)*. Nairobi, Kenya: East African Literature Bureau, 1977.

Knappert, Jan. *Traditional Swahili Poetry: An Investigation Into the Concepts of East African Islam as Reflected in the Utenzi Literature*. Leiden, Netherlands: Brill, 1967.

Knappert, Jan. *Swahili Islamic Poetry, Vol. 1*. Leiden, Netherlands: Brill, 1971.

Knappert, Jan. *Swahili Proverbs*. Burlington, Vermont: University of Vermont, 1997.

Majid al Najdi, Ahmad. *Arab Navigation in the Indian Ocean Before the Coming of the Portuguese*. London, England: The Royal Asiatic Society of Great Britain and Ireland, 1971.

wa Mutiso, Kineene. *The Catharis: Poems*. Seoul, Korea: Shinhan Publishing, 1992.

wa Mutiso, Kineene. *The Hamziyyah Epic: A Detailed Analysis of a Swahili Islamic Epic*. Dar-es-Salaam, Tanzania: University of Dar-es-Salaam, 2005.

Mazrui, Alamin M. and Ibrahim Noor Shariff. *The Swahili: Idiom and Identity of an African People*. Lawrenceville, New Jersey: Africa World Press, 1996.

Menzies, Gavin. *1421: The Year China Discovered America*. New York, New York: Harper Perennial, 2004.

Meredith, Don. *Where the Tigers Were: Travels through Literary Landscapes*. Columbia, South Carolina: University of South Carolina Press, 2001.

Middleton, John. *The World of the Swahili: An African Mercantile Civilization*. New Haven, Connecticut: Yale University Press, 1992.

Mirza, Sarah and Margaret Strobel, eds. *Three Swahili Women: Life Histories from Mombasa, Kenya*. Bloomington: Indiana University Press, 1989.

bin Mwinyi Bakari, Mtoro. *The Customs of the Swahili People: The Desturi Za Waswahili of Mtoro Bin Mwinyi Bakari and other Swahili Persons (Hermeneutics, Studies in the History of Religions*. Berkeley: University of California Press, 1981.

bin Nasir, Sayyid Abdalla bin Ali. *Al Inkishafi: Catechism of a Soul*. (tr. James de Vere Allen) Nairobi, Kenya: East African Literature Bureau, 1977.

Ntarangwi, Mwenda. *Gender, Identity, and Performance: Understanding Swahili Cultural Realities through Song*. Lawrenceville, New Jersey: Africa World Press, 2003.

Romero, Patricia W. *Lamu: History, Society, and Family in an East African Port City (Topics in World History)*. Princeton, New Jersey: Markus Wiener Publishers, 1997.

Ruete, Emily. *Memoirs of an Arabian Princess from Zanzibar (Topics in World History)*. Princeton, New Jersey: Markus Wiener Publishers, 1996.

Sheriff, Abdul, ed. *The History & Conservation of Zanzibar Stone Town (East African Studies)*. Athens, Ohio: Ohio University Press, 1995.

Sheriff, Abdul and Javed Jafferji. *Zanzibar Stone Town: An Architectural Exploration*. Zanzibar, Tanzania: Gallery Publications, 1998.

Snow, Philip. *The Star Raft: China's Encounter with Africa*. Ithaca, New York: Cornell University Press, 1998.

Sing, daughter,
Sing;
Around you are
uncountable tunes,
some sung,
others unsung.

Sing them
to your rhythms:
observe;
listen;
absorb.
Soak yourself;
bathe
in the stream of life,
and then sing.

Sing
simple songs
for the people,
for all to hear,
and learn
and sing
with you.

Micere Githae Mugo,
— Kenyan Poet